New

Directions in

Swiss

Architecture

NEW DIRECTIONS IN ARCHITECTURE

NEW DIRECTIONS IN SWISS ARCHITECTURE
by Jul Bachmann and Stanislaus von Moos

NEW DIRECTIONS IN AFRICAN ARCHITECTURE
by Udo Kultermann

NEW DIRECTIONS IN AMERICAN ARCHITECTURE
by Robert A. M. Stern

NEW DIRECTIONS IN BRITISH ARCHITECTURE
by Royston Landau

NEW DIRECTIONS IN GERMAN ARCHITECTURE
by Gunther Feuerstein

NEW DIRECTIONS IN ITALIAN ARCHITECTURE
by Vittorio Gregotti

NEW DIRECTIONS IN JAPANESE ARCHITECTURE
by Robin Boyd

NEW DIRECTIONS IN LATIN AMERICAN ARCHITECTURE
by Francisco Bullrich

NEW DIRECTIONS IN SOVIET ARCHITECTURE
by Anatole Kopp

JUL BACHMANN

STANISLAUS VON MOOS

NEW DIRECTIONS

IN

SWISS

ARCHITECTURE

GEORGE BRAZILLER   NEW YORK

Translated by Christian Casparis

CONTENTS

LEGEND

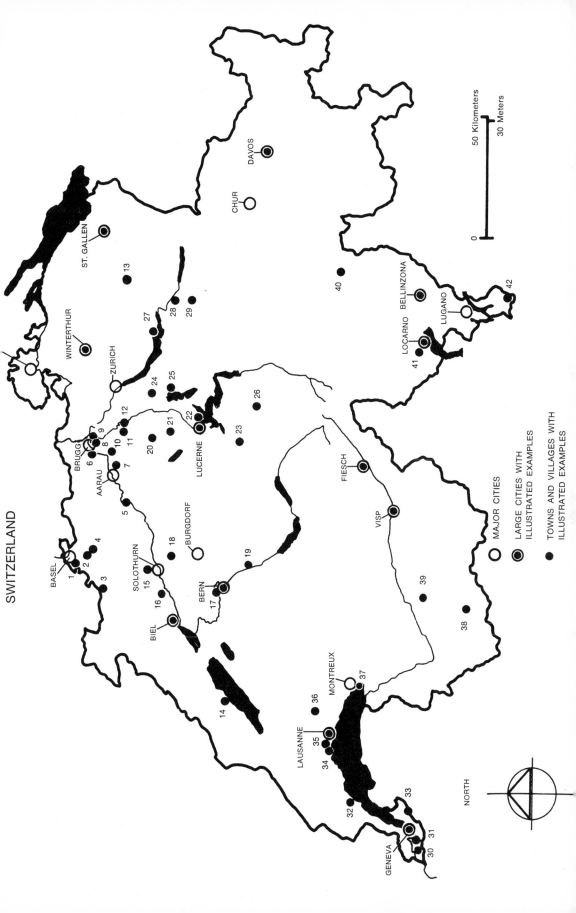

SWITZERLAND

NORTH

50 Kilometers

30 Meters

○ MAJOR CITIES

◉ LARGE CITIES WITH
   ILLUSTRATED EXAMPLES

● TOWNS AND VILLAGES WITH
   ILLUSTRATED EXAMPLES

DAVOS

CHUR

ST. GALLEN

13

WINTERTHUR

ZURICH

27

28

29

24

25

26

40

BELLINZONA

LOCARNO

LUGANO

42

41

BRUGG

9

12

22

23

AARAU

8

10

11

6

20

21

7

LUCERNE

5

BASEL

4

BURGDORF

FIESCH

2

10

18

19

VISP

1

SOLOTHURN

3

15

BERN

16

17

39

BIEL

38

MONTREUX

36

37

LAUSANNE

35

14

34

33

32

GENEVA

31

30

NEW DIRECTIONS IN
SWISS ARCHITECTURE?

ONE is tempted to say: There are none.

In 1955 a booklet titled *Achtung: die Schweiz* (Beware, Switzerland) appeared in Basel. Its authors were the dramatist Max Frisch, who holds a degree in architecture from the E.T.H. (Federal Institute of Technology) in Zurich, the sociologist Lucius Burckhardt, who later became editor of *Werk*, and Markus Kutter, a writer and public relations specialist. They proposed to found a permanent "new city" somewhere in the Swiss Midlands, which would take the place of the National Exhibition planned for 1964 and would not have to be dismantled within a few months. The idea of building a model "new city" was not merely an architect's dream, for it was based on the question of whether there existed in Switzerland any idea or conception of how the nation would shape its future, or whether there was even a national way of life.

One may ask whether over and above Switzerland's excellent machines, chocolate, cheese, and watches, and beyond its famous "neutrality," there is any value which could be defined as specifically Swiss. Is Switzerland with its beautiful and valuable scenery nothing more than a paradise of prosperity, order, and politicoeconomic stability, a playground of the world, an international banking center? Is Switzerland then a purely conservative structure, or does it embody a concept which looks to the future as was the case in 1848 when the Swiss Confederation was established? Will Switzerland retire from history or will it seize and shape, in its own manner, a world that is in the process of rapid change? A national exhibition in the form of a monumental fair could hardly be expected to offer convincing answers to questions such as these. Yet the new Swiss city proposed in 1955 as a model for future urban and regional development as well as for future urban legislation in Switzerland remained a fanciful dream. The idea finally ended in somewhat fruitless legal discussions.

Meanwhile Expo 64, the first Swiss National Exhibition since 1939, took place on the waterfront of Lake Geneva. Some of the best architects of the country built pavilions in which the various aspects of economy, science, culture, art, and even national defense were displayed in a pleasant and tasteful way (*Fig. 1*). Expo 64 dismissed its visitors with the confidence that the decisive problems of Switzerland were solved, or that conditions at least provided for the solution of these problems. A few critical and unanswered questions with which Switzerland has to cope were raised only marginally. These were, for instance, the question of women's suffrage in the country that proudly calls itself "the world's oldest democracy," and the question of the fate of almost one million foreign workers from Italy, Spain, Greece, and Turkey, with whom Switzerland has its own unsolved racial problem.

How is all this related to our question?

Switzerland does not seem to be in the mood to discuss vital issues, to question the present for the sake of the future. Nor does it see fit to change what already exists. As long as domestic affairs function smoothly, the nation's conscience is clear, or at least nearly so.

Switzerland is a peaceful country. The social tensions which threaten the internal peace of neighboring countries barely graze Swiss borders—a testimony to the efficient functioning of the Swiss system. (When large groups of youths recently clashed violently with the police in Zurich, they were not demanding racial equality, demonstrating against an unjust war, or fighting for university reform. What they wanted was a youth center which would not be controlled by "adults.") Of course, at the bottom of such disquietude lies a basic dissatisfaction with the arrogance of the political, economic, and social establishment. But one may well ask whether, within this universal problem of the civilized world today, there are no specifically definable conflicts in Switzerland.

1. Max Bill: "Café de la Presse," Swiss National Exhibition, Lausanne, 1964, roof with view of Lake Geneva.

In short, this picturesque, industrious country is not necessarily the place where, near the 1970's, one would seek new directions in architecture. If present-day Switzerland possesses a "national image," it is an economic, social, and political one rather than an intellectual or cultural one. On no account does this image appear in clear-cut architectural forms as did, for instance, the growing power of the city-states in the Middle Ages, or the economic boom of the American Midwest in the days of the Chicago School. Swiss advantages—freedom of thought, general welfare, social justice, tolerance, and political neutrality—have no particularly representative architectural physiognomy (in fact, they are a good guarantee against any attempt to give Switzerland an architectural face). The centers of social crises, as well as the great economic and intellectual powers which have reformulated planning aims and endeavors, still lie far outside Switzerland. The important building commissions which influence international development have always been handed out in other countries. Thus the Swiss who made a real contribution to world architecture—from Maderno and Borromini (both born in regions which later became parts of Switzerland) to Le Corbusier—naturally worked in Rome or Paris rather than, say, in Lugano or in Zurich.

A Backyard of History: Europe's Meeting Place

In spite of the remarkable productions of creative Swiss minds in many fields, it has been said that Switzerland today is politically and culturally a backyard of history. For this country the time of great crises and conflicts, which question every existing value, has passed. But it has always been a crisis that has forced man into new directions; the Swiss Confederation itself resulted from a crisis. Its present form, well over a century old, represents the attempt to balance permanent domestic and foreign crises. It was preceded in the thirteenth century by the union of the four forest cantons against the Habsburg rule, and in the seventeenth century by a loose federation of independent republics. Today the protracted and bloody throes which finally gave birth to the Swiss Confederation are past. Swiss citizens reap the fruits of welfare and freedom sown by their forefathers. In these circumstances, is it not altogether superfluous to inquire after new directions?

Whether or not Switzerland is culturally and therefore architecturally a backyard, perhaps its peace and security are not only its great danger but also its chance. The country's problems do not offer the necessary stimuli for far-reaching architectural utopias. The revolutionary ideas have already been brought forth by our fathers and grandfathers, and a young architect in Switzerland, even more than elsewhere, is an adapter rather than a creator of architectural principles. However, some interesting speculation in architectural research is being carried out (especially by men like Pascal Hausermann in Geneva, who is proposing agglomerations of egg-shaped plastic houses, or Walter Jonas in Zurich, who for years has worked on his Crater City which has become known throughout the world). The force of present Swiss architecture lies in its close combat with reality rather than in far-reaching strategy. Its contribution is in the practical rather than the theoretical field, in technical and constructional experience rather than creative speculation and imaginative outlooks.

Switzerland seems to offer particularly favorable conditions for the organic development of certain phenomena. In some respects serious work is encouraged by an atmosphere which is not continuously threatened by the troubles of the day. Not only architects have taken advantage of this situation. The stability of conditions has induced many institutions to locate in Switzerland. In Geneva, for instance, are the head secretariat of the International Red Cross (an organization founded, incidentally, by a Swiss) and the European headquarters of the U.N. In addition to Switzerland's famed banking secrecy, there are other reasons for writers, artists, and other private citizens to be tempted by placid Switzerland. At the time of the Dada movement (1916–1922), a "new direction" which could have begun only in a backyard of history, Lenin profited from the advantages of this small neutral country. In a small room in Zurich he formulated his revolutionary theory, and from there he traveled to St. Petersburg in 1917 to take over command of the October Revolution.

Switzerland was a kind of cultural focus in Europe when, culturally and intellectually, a unified Europe no longer existed, while Germany was preparing for World War II and declaring most innovative tendencies "degenerate." In those years various artists, writers, and scientists took refuge in Switzerland. A similar situation had occurred in the nineteenth century when the architect Gottfried Semper fled from the 1848 German Revolution to Switzerland, where he built the large and important main building of the Federal Institute of Technology in Zurich.

During and between the two world wars Switzerland quite involuntarily assumed the function of a kind of authority in questions of environmental design. Ideas thought out elsewhere achieved a valid form there since they met a high level of technical experience and an incorruptible standard of craftsmanship. In this backyard of Europe, people seemed to have time to think conscientiously about and execute the new tasks. Thus it is hardly astonishing that foreign architects who visited Switzerland after World War II encountered a standard of architecture which technically was comparable only to that of Sweden, Finland, or the United States.

In this context we must mention an event closely involving

Switzerland and having worldwide consequences: the founding of C.I.A.M. (*Congrès Internationaux d'Architecture Moderne*) in June 1928, in the castle of La Sarraz, Canton of Vaud. Madame Hélène de Mandrot of Geneva, perhaps following a suggestion of F. T. Gubler, secretary of the Swiss Werkbund, turned to Le Corbusier in Paris with the proposition of arranging a meeting of modern architects from all over the world in her castle. Her idea came at a favorable moment. The rejection in 1927 of Le Corbusier's project for the League of Nations Palace roused all the powers of innovation in the field of architecture. Nothing seemed more appropriate than to gather these loose strands in an international congress. We cannot pursue the activity of C.I.A.M. any further here, but it should be noted that from the start Swiss participants in these congresses played an important role. The first president was Karl Moser, the Swiss contemporary of Berlage and Wagner and the architect of Zurich University and the Church of St. Anthony in Basel. The organization of the congresses lay in the hands of the general secretary, Sigfried Giedion. His architect friends of Zurich, Alfred Roth, Rudolf Steiger, and Werner Moser, assisted him. This kind of international activity naturally established a number of lasting contacts between Switzerland and the world, contacts which were to have an effect on the Swiss architectural scene.

We may add that since 1929, when Hans Girsberger and Willy Boesiger published the first volume of Le Corbusier's *Oeuvre Complète*, Zurich has become a center for publishing and documenting modern architecture; for example, the work of Richard Neutra, Walter Gropius, Alvar Aalto, and José Luis Sert.

If we look at the past, it becomes clear that a close contact with foreign countries is basic to Swiss culture. Since the Middle Ages Switzerland has grown into a politically and socially independent structure. Time and again, because of its somewhat complacent attitude as a neutral country, it has run the risk of isolating itself politically and intellectually from its neighbors. On the other hand, the course of its economic, cultural, and artistic development has always been linked with the adjoining regions. The various parts of the country drew on the heritage of the principalities from which they had dissociated themselves. The medieval cities such as Bern, Basel, or Fribourg with their Gothic minsters are proof of this.

Without its neighbors Switzerland could not have survived economically. Only 30 percent of the area of modern Switzerland is arable or habitable. Apart from water there are no natural resources, nor is there any direct access to the sea. From the beginning there has only been one way to survive: friendship and trade with all the surrounding countries. Negotiation of the neutrality of Switzerland in Vienna, in 1814, only confirmed the country's economic basis of existence. The fact that Switzerland today knows practically no state-enforced import or export restrictions demonstrates that its openness toward all foreign markets is the primary condition of its existence and prosperity.

Culturally Switzerland represents that historic paradox of sharp contrasts peacefully coexisting. With its four languages it cannot be identified with any one of the surrounding cultures but seems rather to consist of one corner each of France, Italy, and Germany. And yet this same country possesses the third highest per capita income in the world, after the United States and Sweden.

After these somewhat diverse remarks about Switzerland in general, we turn to its architectural problems. For this we must take into account the immediate past. In the twenties it was French and German architects who reached new achievements. We think of Le Corbusier's activity, for example his Pessac development near Bordeaux (1925–1926), and the enormous influence of the Bauhaus, as well as enterprises such as the *Weissenhofsiedlung* in Stuttgart (1927), or the housing units by Gropius and his collaborators in Berlin (1929–1930).

The thirties brought Switzerland onto the scene and in fact mark a typical phase in Swiss architecture. In 1930–1932 a group of leading Swiss architects (Ernst Haefeli, Werner Moser, Rudolf Steiger, Emil Roth, Paul Artaria, Carl Hubacher, and Hans Schmidt) built the Werkbund-Siedlung Neubühl in Zurich (*Fig. 2*). Although it is too small to constitute a whole neighborhood unit, it nevertheless includes a school and several types of apartments, allowing the inhabitants to move within the unit according to their changing needs.

A few years later, in 1935, Alfred and Emil Roth, with Marcel Breuer, built the two well-known Doldertal apartments which were commissioned by Sigfried Giedion. G. E. Kidder Smith has rightly observed that since these apartments, housing in Switzerland "has been proper, very well equipped, and beautifully built, but almost totally without architectural spark."[1]

True, the thirties was not only a period of evolution. The upsurge of nazism in Germany encouraged two trends in Swiss architecture. On the one hand, some important work was done in modern architecture. On the other hand, many people believed that the only alternative Switzerland had to offer in the face of the massive "blood and soil" culture propagated by Germany was a national style based on the distinctive features of native Swiss architecture. The art historian Peter Meyer, then editor of *Werk*, justified this trend which later was to be called *Heimatstil* by stating that "modern architecture," which he called "technical style," and *Heimatstil* had their common source in the English Arts and Crafts Movement of the nineteenth century.[2]

The Swiss National Exhibition of 1939, which opened in Zurich a few months before the outbreak of World War II, testified to Switzerland's will for independence. The architectural and artistic consequences of this exhibition, however, proved rather controversial. From 1939 on the Swiss pictured their ideal home as a charming chalet with glowing red geraniums in front of the windows. The National Exhibition showed how regional romanticism was to be fused with more modern elements as developed by Scandinavian architects in order to achieve a "style" both rustic and elegant. In fact, in most cases the Swiss *Heimatstil* interpreted the age-old demand for homeliness in a rather unimaginative fashion. This becomes particularly clear when we compare the industralized piecework in an ordinary Swiss furniture or interior decoration store with Scandinavian handicraft which draws upon a long tradition and yet possesses a distinctly contemporary character. Swiss *Heimatstil* had a remarkable influence on building because it was able to merge comfortably with a tradition of stone and wood construction—techniques which would have been perfectly adaptable to new requirements.

Today one may well argue that the thousands of chalets in Switzerland's alpine vacation resorts are not the worst thing that could happen to the Swiss landscape, compared with some of the modernistic frivolities of our day. However, it is a rather dubious and unsatisfactory experience to see the features of native alpine architecture reappear in the suburban areas of large towns. We may find a so-called typical Grisons stone house peacefully flanked on the

2. Werkbund-Siedlung: *Neubühl, Zurich (Niedelbadstrasse), 1932.*

one side by a chalet that looks like a Bernese alpine dairy farm and on the other—why not?—a villa in a Corbusian style. Both private and cooperative housing of the forties and early fifties are often charmingly equipped with wrought-iron window gratings and sculptured wooden balconies and main entrances.

Building Since 1945: Swiss Architecture and Its Models

After World War II these rather obsolete features lived on quite happily. In the meantime, economic and cultural communication had been revived between Switzerland and its neighbors. With open arms Switzerland greeted the general prosperity which introduced many American features onto the Swiss scene. The last ten years have seen the rapid growth of lavishly equipped shopping centers. Almost every small town boasts of its own glass and steel skyscraper. Many of these, such as Rudolf Meyer's and Guido Keller's new office tower in the center of Aarau, show a remarkable quality of design hardly to be found under similar conditions in the United States.

In order to understand the problems of present-day architecture in Switzerland we must examine its socioeconomic background.

The birth of modern architecture in the twenties has been closely associated with the development of mass production for mass consumption. Mass production of standardized elements is still an aim, though an often neglected one, of the building industry. Switzerland has relatively little to offer in this most important field, for many reasons. The Swiss free-trade system encourages the development of isolated initiative in the sphere of standardized and prefabricated building elements. In certain areas large-scale entrepreneurs have taken command, but the limited market in Switzerland has led to the failure of several businesses producing quite interesting industrialized building elements. In fact, prefabrication is, at present, not synonymous with low-cost building. Only if it is undertaken on a national or even European scale will building with industrialized elements be more economical than building with conventional means. The chances of a successful prefabrication system today are further diminished by the fact that conventional building recently has been considerably economized by comprehensive and advanced programming systems of the building process.

Not only economic but also sociological factors condition the development of standardized systems. In Switzerland, as well as in other countries, building to a great extent has become an object of individual creation and choice rather than mass production and mass consumption. Swiss society is increasingly involved in service industries. Values symbolizing the status of an individual, a commercial enterprise, or a political community are becoming more and more prominent. Current architecture with its unlimited constructional possibilities offers an arsenal of tempting solutions for every purpose.

The abundance of means, enhanced by prosperity, represents in fact a serious danger for the visual quality of our surroundings. Trivial Swiss architecture of the past years shows how difficult it has become to create a simple and decent form for an everyday purpose. It is now becoming more and more evident that restriction of means and serious experimentation with new constructional principles are still a better premise for visual quality than mere architectural "inspiration."

During the last twenty years Swiss architecture has returned to the mainstream of the functional tradition. This trend has been considerably enhanced by the important influence of the postwar work of the great master-builders. Le Corbusier exerted by far the strongest influence. His first collaborators were Swiss, and there were times when, in his atelier at 35 rue de Sèvres, Paris, Swiss-German was heard more than French. Among these collaborators Alfred Roth and later Bernhard Hoesli became most successful teachers in the Department of Architecture of the E.T.H. in Zurich.

The presence of Le Corbusier's work is felt throughout postwar architecture. The polemical vocabulary of his books still forms the basis for architectural and urbanistic debates. Many Swiss architects use the Modulor as a natural aid. Of course not many achievements

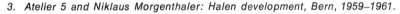

3. *Atelier 5 and Niklaus Morgenthaler: Halen development, Bern, 1959–1961.*

in recent Swiss architecture embody a synthesis comparable to that unity of reason and imagination, of social involvement and visual force realized by Le Corbusier himself. Certain work done by the Atelier 5 (Erwin Frey, Samuel Gerber, Rolf Hesterberg, Hans Hostettler, Alfredo Pini, and Fritz Thormann) or by architects such as Dolf Schnebli marks a most interesting adaptation of Le Corbusier's ideas within specifically Swiss problems of housing (*Figs. 3, 49–50*).

What impressed the majority of Le Corbusier's Swiss admirers was above all the sculptural vehemence of his art. It is through extreme subjectivity that some of Le Corbusier's late works arrived at their objective validity. Here of course lies the danger of his followers, in the hands of whom Le Corbusier's style often dries up into a more or less hectic but essentially dessicated formalism. In the late fifties the sculptural possibilities of concrete were emphasized in a hitherto unknown prodigality by the architects Walter M. Förderer, Rolf G. Otto, and Hans Zwimpfer. In fact, much of the concrete architecture of the last several years that aspires to monumentality is openly inspired by Förderer; for many architects, his early projects served as a starting point for their own sculptural ambitions. In recent buildings by Förderer or architects such as Otto Glaus this dramatically petrified dissolution of architectural form seems to have reached a definite end (*Fig. 4*).

On the other hand, the purity of form as achieved by Mies van der Rohe has become a goal for many younger Swiss architects.

4. Walter M. Förderer: Catholic church, Lichtensteig, under construction, model.

Here a highly spiritual conception of architecture has been caught up in a sense for precision, refinement in construction, and luxurious detailing which for generations has been a proudly coveted virtue in this land of watchmakers. It was the experience in Mies's Chicago office that opened the eyes of the young Basel architect, Werner Blaser, to the beauties of Japanese architecture.[3] Without being actual disciples of Mies, architects such as Bruno and Fritz Haller, Franz Füeg, and others have made considerable achievements in the line of Miesian architecture (*Fig. 5*). In some projects the Hallers as well as Füeg (*Figs. 122–123*) seem impressed by the "classical" character of Miesian designs with their axes and symmetrical layouts, but in their most suggestive works they emphasize more the purity of form and the possibilities of standardization and flexibility which are offered by this architectural idiom (*cf. Figs. 90–91*). In the work of the young Hans R. Bader a suggestive creative enrichment of this crystalline architecture appears, especially Bader's juxtaposition of serving and served spaces in his recent school projects (*Fig. 86*). When a sense of proportion is coupled with an adequacy of means and materials the results will often attain a high level of quality. Nevertheless, among the innumerable curtain-wall facades of the last fifteen years there are but a few examples in which simplicity represents a value rather than the mere lack of ideas.

There is another great architect to whose creative impulse Swiss architects responded even more vividly: the Finnish master, Alvar Aalto, who recently built his apartments on the waterfront of Lake Lucerne (*Figs. 6–7*). Aalto's architecture possesses qualities which are quite naturally akin to the Swiss character. While Frank Lloyd Wright and Le Corbusier projected their ideas lavishly into the future, Aalto conceived the house of the present. While Le Corbusier envisaged vast urban complexes, Aalto preferred to deal with small, surveyable communities. In his hands wood and brick, the traditional elements of native building, were transformed into a differentiated means of architectural and spatial expression. Similar results, though on a smaller scale and with a typically Swiss emphasis on constructional perfection, have been achieved by architects such as

5. Bruno and Fritz Haller: Factory, Münsingen, 1963.

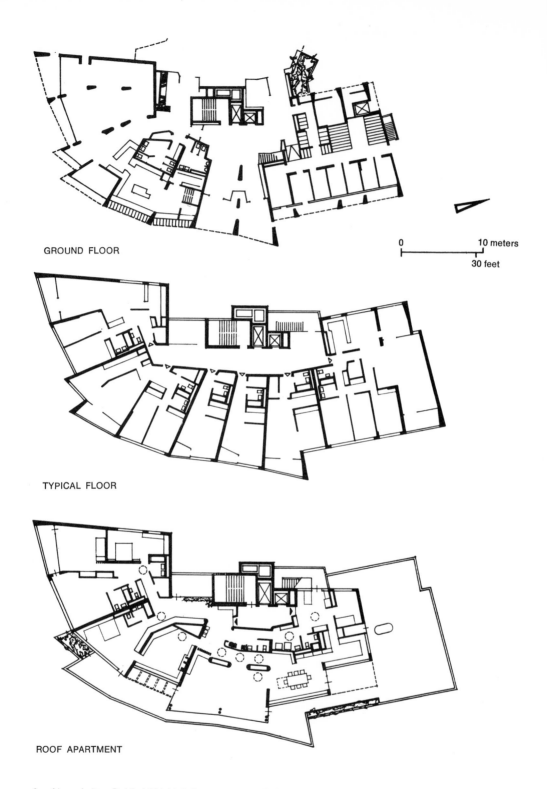

GROUND FLOOR

0   10 meters
|_____|
                     30 feet

TYPICAL FLOOR

ROOF APARTMENT

6. *Alvar Aalto: Schönbühl highrise apartment building, Lucerne, 1965–1967, plans.*

7. *Schonbuhl highrise apartment building. On the left, shopping center by Alfred Roth.*

Ernst Gisel (*Fig. 8*), who was never actually connected with Aalto. Significantly, the latest terrace developments in Swiss architecture, such as that by Team 2000 and Hans Ulrich Scherer near Brugg (*Figs. 55–56*), find their classic prototype in Aalto's little-known Kauttua apartments of 1938–1939. Not by chance do we find among Aalto's collaborators more architects from Switzerland than from any other foreign country. Among these Eduard Neuenschwander (*Fig. 9*) and Ulrich Stucky, for instance, have successfully applied their Scandinavian experiences in Switzerland.

For centuries Swiss architecture was slow to catch up with the change of styles that occurred in the great cultural centers of Europe. This lack of immediate contact with European artistic developments enhanced the formation of regional building types which are almost as numerous and varied as the different Swiss dialects. Today, however, in the age of mass media, this kind of retardation of style no longer exists. It was in the unperturbed bourgeois town of Bern in 1968 that the American artist Christo wrapped up for the first time an entire building, the Kunsthalle, in an enormous plastic bag.

But one may notice how little, in fact, Switzerland has been affected by that "new direction" in postwar architecture defined by Nikolaus Pevsner as "New Historicism"[4] and sarcastically named "playboy architecture" by Sigfried Giedion in the latest editions of his *Space, Time, and Architecture.*[5] Swiss architects until now have hardly been involved in the kind of frivolous flirt with the muses of historically remote European architecture which endows so many recent buildings in the United States with their sophisticated aura. Nor did analogous but more substantial tendencies in Italy, as represented by the Torre Velasca in Milan, have any considerable echo in Switzerland.

In this context the problem of the modern architect's dialogue with tradition arises. With every new building to be built in a traditional environment the architect is faced with the alternative of either stating his point in clearly modern terms as a dialectic antithesis to the environment, or trying to start a friendly conversation with what he finds there.

This problem will, in fact, become one of the foremost questions of Swiss architecture in years to come. Switzerland, undamaged by the bombs of two world wars, has to find a way out of the dilemma in which most of its medieval city centers find themselves. On the one hand they are threatened with decay—many have as a consequence become deteriorated living areas—and on the other hand they are threatened even more by prosperity. There are cases where extraordinary medieval surroundings are perverted by sophisticated shopping areas. In Lucerne, for instance, large department stores duck behind facades which try to imitate the rhythm of their medieval

8. Ernst Gisel: Park theater, Grenchen, 1954.

9. Eduard Neuenschwander: Ramibühl High School, Zurich, under construction, site plan.

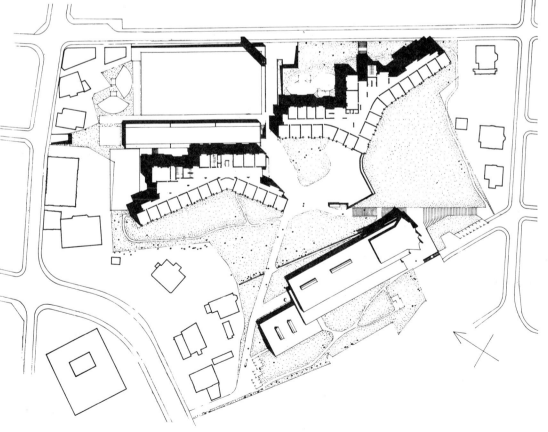

neighborhood. Controversial problems which touch the very essence of Switzerland's architectural heritage, such as the adaptation of city centers, can be handled only by thorough urban planning principles. Any mere architectural approach is bound to remain a matter of cosmetics.

True as this is, architects are nevertheless faced with the task of building within traditional surroundings. In general, one may note that in Swiss cities as well as in the country the idea of a clear dialectic dialogue is, if at all, realized on a much higher architectural level than the idea of adaptation, which in most cases is synonymous with a renunciation of architectural ambition and is executed in terms of a rather obsolete *Heimatstil*.

The Tours de Carouge (*Figs. 39–40, see also p. 53*), offer an example of an organic urban expansion in terms of an almost dramatic juxtaposition of old and new. On the other hand, the transformation of shops and restaurants in the old town of Zurich, at the Neumarkt, shows a creative effort toward a sensitive adaptation of the traditional to new needs (*Fig. 10*). By merely clearing

10. *Fritz Schwarz: Shop renewal at the Neumarkt in the old town of Zurich, 1964.*

backyards a true enrichment of the urban scale can be achieved, as demonstrated by the "Rosenhof" in Zurich (*Fig. 11*). However, some work done by architects like Fritz Schwarz, Wolfgang Behles, or Manuel Pauli, in spite of its interesting outlook, is limited to a somewhat sceneographic effect that is fully justified in the charming Children's Zoo at Rapperswil (*Figs. 108–109*), but would seem to be rather dubious in enterprises on an urban scale.

"Building as a Process"

Louis Sullivan's well-known dictum, "form follows function," has remained one of the basic convictions of modern architecture, although of course the concept of function has changed considerably since Sullivan's day. Today this principle is becoming more and more questionable.

In an interesting treatise, *Bauen ein Prozess*, Lucius Burckhardt and Walter M. Forderer have recently criticized the method of classifying buildings according to their purpose. They rightly observe that the more a building is fitted to a specific function the smaller the

11. Benedikt Huber: "Rosenhof," clearing of an urban backyard, Zurich, 1966–1967.

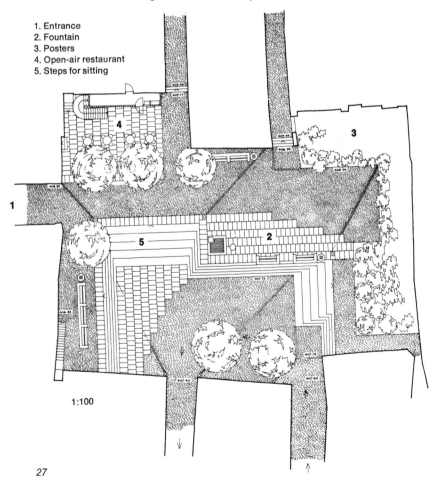

1. Entrance
2. Fountain
3. Posters
4. Open-air restaurant
5. Steps for sitting

1:100

chance of its adaptability to unpredictable future needs. Despite the fact that the free ground plan and the free facade belong to the early principles of Corbusian architecture, architects know well that old buildings can be much more adaptable to changing requirements than modern, strictly functional ones. Moreover, due to the current mechanisms of decision-making, the isolation and separate handling of building projects such as schools, community centers, churches, and recreation centers does not correspond with the actual requirements of a society whose structure is constantly fluctuating. This is why the demand for a planning which envisages processes rather than isolated measures, and an adequate mixture of functions rather than a differentiation of them, becomes increasingly imperative.

Burckhardt and Förderer see their arguments as clearly contrasting with the ideals of the functionalist tradition. But they are not the first to demand a flexible and variable architecture. One may recall that Le Corbusier, as early as 1914, suggested a constructional system which would enable its inhabitants to arrange their own interiors and facades according to their changing individual needs.[6] Le Corbusier expressed the same idea seventeen years later in his famous Plan Obus for Algiers and in his "growing museum." In Algiers the different levels of the huge serpentine complex haphazardly comprise a great variety of spontaneous structures (the same conception has recently been adopted by Kenzo Tange in his well-known Tokyo Bay project). One may also recall that as early as 1930 the German architect Hans Hilbersheimer conceived his "growing house," inspired by the important projects of Walter Gropius and Marcel Breuer in the Bauhaus years. Perhaps "new directions" in architecture will have to look back to such early contributions toward the problem of flexibility and variability and start where they left off. The more advanced theoretical research in this field has been done by the Atelier des Architectes Associés (Atelier AAA) in Lausanne. These architects are proposing large vertical frameworks in which boxes of single living units are to fit like drawers; above and below the traditional units are to be open spaces which will make future changes or enlargements possible.

Of course flexibility is not only a question of advanced prefabrication systems, but must also be considered in the light of a prevailing readiness of people to invest time and money in the building of their individual houses. People have a right to participate creatively in forming their environment. From this point of view, the spontaneous do-it-yourself architecture in Swiss urban outskirts or "Bidonvilles" possesses a human touch much superior to the perfect design of so many cooperative housing blocks (*Fig. 12*). By encouraging their commissioners to participate creatively and extensively in the building process, the Geneva architects Frei, Hunziker, and Hunziker are making an interesting advance into the field of architectural psychology and experimentation. But of course in its present stage such Rousseauism is far from offering a pertinent answer to immediate large-scale building problems.

Walter M. Forderer, the architect of the well-known Swiss Graduate School of Economics and Administration (1960–1963) in St. Gallen, whose sculptural idiom may be considered the "new direction" of Swiss architecture of the fifties, has since become a most eloquent advocate of the mixture of functions, the simultaneity and complexity of functions within a single building complex. In Förderer's work, however, this interpenetration of uses does not result in anonymous forms as might be expected but in a rather pathetic image of a hierarchic community—an immovable and incorruptible image which has a somewhat absolutistic character, as his project for the community center in Hérémence shows. As the Viennese architect Friedrich Achleitner has stated, the trouble with this kind of architecture lies in the fact that "the ephemeral and ever-changing [functions a building has to fulfill] is cast in concrete in the form of a momentary and subjective interpretation."[7]

It is questionable whether flexibility and variability can be appropriately expressed in visual terms by an essentially hierarchical architectural approach. Once again it may be useful to look at anonymous everyday buildings which seldom claim architectural dignity. Many Swiss *Gewerbehäuser* (city-owned establishments, temporarily let to workshops or small industrial enterprises) illustrate

12. *Typical small plot in a Swiss suburban area.*

admirably what we mean by flexibility and variability in building. In industrial plants such principles have been a matter of course for many years. Industrial plants are increasingly avoiding specialization although they are highly equipped with basic utilities such as water, electricity, and compressed air. This principle of planning has recently been adapted to school design. In particular, Luigi Snozzi's project for the Teachers Training College in Locarno (*Fig. 13*), and Alfons Barth's and Hans Zaugg's high school of Frauenfeld, near Winterthur, exemplify this. One might also think of Dolf Schnebli's project for Washington University in St. Louis, which is focused on the possibility of future change.

The demand for coping with the elements of space and time—a method involving flexibility—and for mixing different functions have become prominent not only in building complexes but also in urbanism. In the field of urbanism Switzerland is once more a country where one encounters little experimentation. As a matter of fact, the problem of urbanism in all its aspects, as put forth in *Achtung: die Schweiz*, has not been tackled. Achievements in urbanism consist of piecework rather than comprehensive planning.

When Jane Jacobs violently attacked the urbanistic principles of C.I.A.M., she based her argument on recent examples of American urban renewal. Swiss examples could not have served her purpose. Switzerland has produced some quite convincing adaptations of the principles of functional differentiation in planning. The "Radiant City" may prove a disaster for people not used to this kind of living together in vast masses. On the other hand it appears to be a quite workable habitat for a relatively highly civilized urban society as encountered in Switzerland. However, such gigantic housing complexes as the satellite town Cite du Lignon in Geneva, with its uniform facade extending more than a kilometer, seriously question the human scale of an urban environment (*Figs. 41–42*). In any case, the experiences after the first building phase of Cité du Lignon prevented the execution of the project in its originally intended dimensions.

In Switzerland, where every city is hopelessly congested by traffic, the separation of traffic ways and the creation of pedestrian areas are prominent issues in urban planning. It will be necessary, however, to balance this kind of functional differentiation by a new mixture of functions in the areas of working and living, in order to transform bedroom communities (*Schlafstädte*) into self-contained living centers. Moreover, solving the problem of the town centers depends on an adequate mixture of urban functions.

What are the formal implications of this developing concept of flexibility and variability in architecture and planning?

One aspect of this change can easily by recognized if we compare Le Corbusier's Unité d'habitation with projects such as his slope

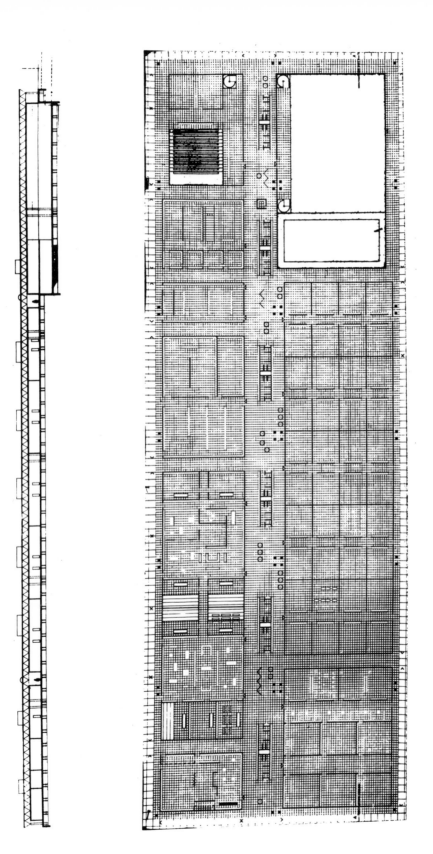

13. Luigi Snozzi (with Walter van Euw): Project for Teachers Training College, Locarno, 1967, elevation and plan.

development of Roq et Rob in southern France. The facade of the Unité d'habitation can be compared with the facade of a Renaissance palazzo in its organization as a pictorial unity. A slope development which forms a crust over the landscape is not perceived as such a unity. It dissolves into a free agglomeration of cellular elements. In fact, recent Swiss terrace layouts no longer have any facade. The Grüzefeld development in Winterthur by Fred Cramer, Werner Jaray, and Claude Paillard is experienced as a system of sequences, progressions of individual cellular units and open spaces, rather than as a compact entity (*Figs. 47–48*). Schools do not appear lined up as street-fronts but as detached, free agglomerations of class-room units often presented in the form of free-standing boxes. From this point of view such utterly different designs as the French School in Geneva by Georges Candilis and Arthur Bugna (*Figs. 96–97*) or, the junior high school in Locarno by Dolf Schnebli (*Figs. 98–99*) show a definite kinship.

Planning in a Democracy

In Switzerland, which has the highest population density in Europe in relation to its habitable and arable space (363 inhabitants per square kilometer), people are moving closer and closer together. In the larger urban areas this is drastically demonstrated by daily traffic jams.

Friction is aggravated on all levels by the democratic structure of Swiss society and by the intricate subdivision of property and administrative competence. In the process of the final shaping of a national highway network, government planning boards find them-selves facing a rather frustrating situation when trying to cope with all the parties involved. Even official Swiss circles are discussing more seriously the demand for a new definition of real estate prop-erty. Although lawyers and politicians are far from offering any pertinent solutions, they realize that present and future needs can hardly be met within the existing framework.

What are we facing?

Conscientious planning must meet the necessity of ensuring an equilibrium between the constants of nature and the variables of civilization. Nature is not inexhaustible. Its resources must be kept available for an ever-increasing population. Yet the rapid growth of industry and of habitation in the Midlands considerably diminishes these natural and agricultural resources. Water and air are in danger. Although considerable efforts have been made to create large water purification plants, more efforts are necessary.

By a federal law of 1902, wooded areas, which cover one fourth of the area of Switzerland, must be maintained. Such measures help prevent chaos, but they are often insufficient for improving the visual quality of the landscape. Careless corruption of the landscape insults the eye. Every interference with the natural scenery or historical heritage endangers Switzerland's image as an international vacation resort.

The landscape and architectural heritage not only guarantee tourist attraction but also form a precious part of the life of Swiss citizens. Nevertheless, rapid structural change is affecting the old towns and villages. Traditional urban and rural living patterns no longer coincide with the needs of industrialized society. In most cases preservation can be effective only if the buildings, settlements, and landscapes preserved are given new functions. In Basel, many government offices now occupy the old patrician mansions of the town center. Throughout the country schools, colleges, or mental homes are found within the walls of former monasteries which were dissolved in the last century.

New highrise buildings, highways, bridges, dams, and high-tension electricity towers give the Swiss landscape an entirely new scale. Disappointing results, such as the fanciful reinforced concrete caprices of National Highway No. 2 in the Tessin, appear as often as examples in which engineering forms dramatically enrich the scenery, such as the most impressive dams in the Alps (*Fig. 19*) or the viaduct of National Highway No. 4 near the Chateau du Chillon.

A federal planning institution that coordinates efforts toward a sensible development of Switzerland does not exist yet. When around 1947 Sigfried Giedion proposed the creation of a department for architect-planners at the E.T.H., his colleagues did not take him seriously. Finally in 1961 the Institute for Communal, Regional, and National Planning (Institut fur Orts-, Regional- und Landesplanung, or O.R.L.) was begun at the E.T.H. Its purpose is scientific research in this field and the formulation of directives for future urban and regional development in Switzerland. However, these directives are not legally binding. The Swiss federal system with its broad communal autonomy is a serious impediment to any large-scale planning. Since the citizen votes whether or not to accept a planning project, it is on the communal level that planning policy is most likely to be established. For regional planning, the cantons, which still jealously guard their regional autonomy, can be induced to follow the directives of the O.R.L. only by appropriate federal subsidies.

One may argue whether planning from small-scale to large-scale is not the wrong way round. Only in view of the whole can a planning measure prove its suitability. Quite often, under the present circumstances, a nice housing area which is perfectly situated within a communal planning pattern is cut in two by a national highway. However, inductive planning policy may have its advantages, for every citizen has to face planning ideas within the limits of his community. When the layout of a new highway is under discussion many a citizen will publicly offer his "professional" advice. Indeed, such constant confrontation with planning problems could be excellent experience for a competent dealing with large-scale projects.

Who Is Building Switzerland?

There are two mainstreams in present Swiss building. On the one hand, a vast amount of trivial architecture is erected by powerful housing cooperatives and general building contractors. In this area Swiss building is sound, quite expensive, and rather uninspired.

However, there is a sphere of architectural activity where an ever-increasing demand for originality, fancifulness, and caprice may be discerned. Here inspiration seems to know no limit. In fact, originality has become a kind of first-ranked professional virtue especially in church design but also in schools or private houses.

These two tendencies result from the particular conditions of architectural practice in Switzerland. First, the architect's title is not legally protected. Anyone who feels the vocation or, as occurs more frequently, wants to make easy money can call himself an architect. It is these people who are partly to blame for the unhealthy speculation which has driven real estate prices to unparalleled heights. Yet it would be fatal to allow only certified architects to practice, since many of Switzerland's most distinguished architects did not study at any of the three government schools of architecture, but studied and gained their first experience in the offices of leading architects. Forderer, for instance, after his career as a sculptor worked in the office of Hermann Baur, the doyen of modern architecture in Basel.

The other factor which conditions Swiss architectural practice is the architectural competition. For public buildings of some importance a competition is held in which every tax-paying architect of the community has an equal chance to win and receive the commission. Usually these competitions are judged not only by the local authorities but also by a number of distinguished and well-known Swiss architects. Without this practice many a talented young Swiss architect would remain unknown. If public buildings generally attain a high artistic standard it is mainly because of this democratic method.

But like many democratic methods competitions also have their drawbacks. For instance, a few years ago Basel proudly announced that in ten years fifty schools had been built by almost as many architects. Such an achievement may admirably suit the interests of architects and the established building industry. Does it also suit the community's need for appropriate and economical school building? Some cantons have since turned to long-term and comprehensive planning of their school and hospital building projects.

Many view the tendency toward increasing architectural diversity (which so often ends in mere individuality and originality, as in church architecture) as the natural expression of liberal, multifaceted Swiss society. However, this diversity is not so much a need of the society as a result of the competitive principle. It is conditioned by the desire to produce a project which is sure to attract the jury's attention and to fulfill the commissioner's demand for nonconformity. In any case, the explanation of such phenomena should not be taken as synonymous with their justification.

A word must be said about Swiss schools of architecture.

Many of the best architects in Switzerland never graduated from an official institution. By no means have Swiss schools of architecture, especially the E.T.H., always been in the vanguard of international architectural development. In the thirties and forties—the years of the local *Heimatstil*—many professors considered men like Le Corbusier, Gropius, and Mies van der Rohe as interesting representatives of a remote past—the twenties—but rather irrelevant to the immediate present. After World War II when Europe reopened its borders the message of architects such as Le Corbusier, Aalto, and others came as an unexpected and striking revelation to many young Swiss architects.

Today official architectural instruction in this country—at the Department of Architecture of the E.T.H. in Zurich, at the E.P.U.L. (Ecole Polytechnique de l'Universite de Lausanne), and at the E.A.U.G. (Ecole d'Architecture de l'Université de Genève)—is relatively open-minded. At the E.T.H. the past fifteen years have seen several fundamental changes in the curriculum. They all aim at making architectural training more flexible and more open to present-day intellectual, artistic, and sociological issues. Students have a voice in setting up the curriculum, and no particular "trend" is taught. From a certain stage in his studies the student is free to choose his teachers from among the faculty.

In a democratic country a school of architecture rightly sees its duty as imparting to its students the necessary, technical, artistic, and administrative knowledge rather than imposing a certain stylistic approach. Swiss schools of architecture, especially the E.T.H., are respected for their solid technical, constructional, and administrative instruction which gives the student architect insight into many social and human implications of his work that are often neglected in purely architectural debates. The Swiss architect has comparatively numerous functions and tasks to fulfill in society. He not only is responsible for the initial overall sketches and finishing touches, but he also works out and controls the entire project from the first sketches down to the most intricate technical details and even the calculation of costs.

Today almost 20 percent of the architecture students at the E.T.H. are foreigners, mostly Europeans. Some of them live in the house which Alfred Roth, the former dean of the Department of Architecture, recently built for himself and his students (*Figs. 14–15*). In Switzerland architectural instruction as a whole is trying to realize a truly Swiss idea: the creation of a democratic forum, where an international dialogue can take place under favorable conditions.

Swiss Builders in the World

For centuries the most renowned Swiss-born architects and builders have developed their faculties outside their country, from Carlo Maderno, the architect of the facades of St. Peter's in Rome, to O. H. Ammann, who built or was consultant for the George Washington, Golden Gate, Bronx-Whitestone and Verrazano-Narrows bridges in the United States.

The most famous architect born in Switzerland is undoubtedly Le Corbusier (1887–1965). His career is a telling example of the fate of a genius in a small state. Until the age of thirty he was active in his native town, La Chaux-de-Fonds, a watchmakers' city in French-speaking western Switzerland. With his friends and his teacher

14. Alfred Roth: Architect's home with student apartments, Zurich, 1960, plans.

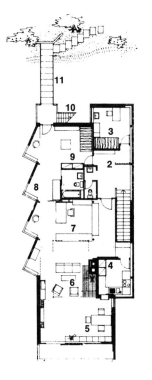
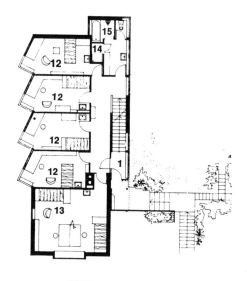

TOP FLOOR   INTERMEDIATE FLOOR

1. Main entrance   9. Bedroom
2. Vestibule   10. Stairs to terrace
3. Guest room   11. Passerelle to garden
4. Kitchen   12. Single student rooms
5. Dining area   13. Double student room
6. Fireplace   14. Shower
7. Work area   15. Bath
8. Projecting molding

Charles L'Eplattenier, who helped found the French-speaking section of the Swiss Werkbund, he contributed much toward turning the new section of the La Chaux-de-Fonds School of Arts and Crafts into an international center for the regeneration of arts and crafts. This would have been a school to be mentioned along with the School of Nancy, where Victor Prouvé was active, or even with Henry van de Velde's Grossherzogliche Sächsische Kunstgewerbeschule in Weimar, which later became the Bauhaus. However, local administrators halted this promising venture with the typically Swiss argument: How will the graduates of this school later earn their living? We do not want artists and designers. We want jewelers, engravers, and chasers for our local industry. L'Eplattenier and his young collaborators resigned. Charles Edouard Jeanneret, who was later to call

15. *Architect's home with student apartments, Zurich.*

himself Le Corbusier, carried out one more commission, a house in La Chaux-de-Fonds. But soon the small town was too narrow for him, and in 1917 he moved to Paris permanently.

It is not tragic that Le Corbusier left his hometown when he did. Had he stayed on, he would have developed into an excellent architect of the higher bourgeoisie of Neuchâtel but hardly into the architectural innovator he became. True to its long-standing tradition, Paris provided the proper scale for the young architect's creative impulse and also offered him the experiences and acquaintances necessary to ignite the spark of inspiration. Only in Paris could Charles Edouard Jeanneret have become Le Corbusier.

What is tragic, however, is that in later years Swiss authorities not once commissioned their famous countryman to erect a public building on Swiss soil. Le Corbusier's only building commissioned by Swiss authorities stands in Paris in the Cité Universitaire. Apart from his early works in La Chaux-de-Fonds, Le Corbusier built only three buildings in Switzerland: the tiny villa for his parents on Lake Geneva (1923–1925), the "Clarté" apartments in Geneva (1930–1931), and the exhibition pavilion, Centre Le Corbusier, in Zurich (1964–1967) (*Fig. 16*). With this pavilion the art gallery owner Heidi Weber tried persistently to compensate for part of the disgrace that surrounds the relation between Le Corbusier and Switzerland. Other than the city of Zurich, which lent the building plot, no official authority helped realize this project.

Although the case of Le Corbusier is undoubtedly the most unusual, it is by no means the only case of a modern Swiss architect who found his field of activity in a foreign country. The same is true of Le Corbusier's cousin, Pierre Jeanneret (1896–1967). Not only did he have a decisive part in all of Le Corbusier's buildings until 1940 as first chief architect, but he was also the leading builder of Chandigarh.

Another architect from Geneva, like Jeanneret, is William Lescaze who with George Howe built the Philadelphia Savings Fund Society Building (1931–1932), the first modern office skyscraper in the United States. The Basel architect Hans Schmidt was engaged in urban planning in Russia in the thirties, and since 1956 he has been active in East Germany. Max Bill, the Swiss painter, architect, and product designer who studied at the Dessau Bauhaus, founded the School of Design (Hochschule fur Gestaltung) in Ulm, Germany in 1955. Nor must we forget O. H. Ammann, who built or was advisor for the longest suspension bridges in the United States.

In this context we must mention another man who is closely connected with the development of modern architecture—Sigfried Giedion. With a typically Swiss blend of pride and self-criticism he wrote a brilliant introduction to his country entitled "Switzerland or the Forming of an Idea" for G. E. Kidder Smith's *Switzerland Builds*. When Giedion, a former student of Heinrich Wölfflin, was appointed

16. Le Corbusier (Travès and Rebutato, Paris, execution): Exhibition pavilion (Centre Le Corbusier), Zurich, 1964–1967, view from the north.

17. André Studer (with Jean Hentsch): Arab development, Casablanca, 1954–1956.

professor at Harvard University in 1938, he was known in the German-speaking world as the man who had written the best book on classicism and on the iron and reinforced concrete architecture of France. In his own country, however, as general secretary of C.I.A.M., Giedion had burnt his fingers as a result of his resolute support for the cause of contemporary architecture and art. Only in America did he find the intellectual scope he required for writing his important works on modern architecture and on the rise of mechanization (*Space, Time, and Architecture* and *Mechanization Takes Command*). Although he found life in Switzerland much more suitable than life in the United States, he remained aware of the fact that the leap into the New World was the essential prerequisite for formulating his ideas and gaining an audience for them.

The list of those Swiss who achieved fame in a foreign country can be considerably extended. It includes Paul Klee, who grew up in Bern; the Bernese teacher Johannes Itten, originator of the famous preliminary course (*Vorkurs*) at the Weimar Bauhaus; and Alberto Giacometti, who became, with his mature works, the artistic representative of existentialism. As a matter of fact there are only a few famous Swiss of this century who made their name in the world while working in Switzerland. Among these we note the engineer Robert Maillart. Although he was active in Russia for a time, his principal works are in Switzerland (see p. 41). Yet he met unusual resistance. At the E.T.H. he was hardly taken seriously. Some cantonal building authorities vigorously objected to the construction of his "puff-pastry bridges" which today have made Swiss engineering skill famous. At the time of his death in 1940 he was a man little known in his own country.

If one asks young Swiss architects such as Ernst Gisel, André Studer, Dolf Schnebli or the members of Atelier 5 what they consider their most important achievements, they point out works done in foreign countries. Gisel is responsible for a part of the Markisches Viertel in Berlin, and Atelier 5 is projecting large student residences in Stuttgart, along with their other developments in Germany and Britain (*Fig. 53*). André Studer has carried out remarkable housing projects for Arabs in Morocco (*Fig. 17*) comparable to some work done by Candilis and Woods. Dolf Schnebli is the creator of the interesting project for Washington University in St. Louis (cf. p.30). Finally, Niklaus Morgenthaler, who in the fifties was mainly responsible for the Halen development in Bern (*Figs. 3, 49–50*), is now the leading advocate for humane and efficient slum clearance methods in Chicago.

TOWARD A BETTER
ENVIRONMENT

Work and Traffic

SIGFRIED GIEDION has defined construction of the nineteenth century as "the subconscious of architecture."[12] One may well ask how far this definition is adaptable to present-day industrial and technical building. Present constructional means do not offer an entirely new conception of space, as did the iron and glass constructions of the nineteenth century. However, some important ideas and concepts, such as flexibility and variability, which have now found their way into architectural and planning discussions, have been applied to industrial architecture for years. Thus it may be useful once again to look back on the development of industrial and engineering building.

Today there is basically no stylistic contrast between industrial and engineering building and the other categories of architecture dealt with in this book. Of course, some difference in creative approach remains. There is little room for merely formalistic eccentricities in a purely technical building, although often a considerable effort is made to invest such a building with a high-quality architectural design. Industrial building, even if executed without any architectural ambition, today possesses a sort of decency and discretion which has become rather rare in other fields of architecture more prone to a kind of architectural show business. In industrial building the individuality of the architect is secondary to the actual work. It is here that we find primary architectural phenomena based on what Le Corbusier defined as "essential attitudes" (*attitudes essentielles*) in speaking about rustic architecture and its lesson for the modern architect.

Switzerland with its sharply broken terrain was the birthplace of alpine funiculars, suspension railways, and many impressive bridges. At the beginning of this century the engineer Robert Maillart opened new perspectives in modern reinforced concrete bridge construction. The Salginatobel bridge in Schiers (1929–1930), the Schwandbach bridge (1933) and the nearby Rossgraben bridge between Hinterfultigen and Schonentannen (1932), and the Arve bridge between Versey and Geneva (1936), are the pride of modern Swiss engineering. Today the planning of new highways still creates many opportunities for extensive engineering, for instance in the long-neglected expansion of the national highway network, which is to extend about 900 miles.

18. *Elektro-Watt, Inc., Zurich: Ventilation shafts of the San Bernardino tunnel, Grisons, 1967.*

19. *Mauvoisin dam, Valais, aerial view.*

While in Maillart's day the shape of the supporting arch was a constituent element of the static stability of a bridge, today prestressed concrete makes it possible to construct large slabs whose stability is independent from the form of the vertical supports. This is shown by the gigantic viaduct above Montreux near the Château du Chillon, where industrial prefabrication methods are ingeniously employed. There are many other examples of imaginative design in highway construction. When crossing the San Bernardino Pass between Bellinzona and Chur one encounters strange structures beside the road (*Fig. 18*); these are not modern churches but in fact large snow-protected ventilation shafts for the road-tunnel which passes below.

The largest and most sensational building feats are carried out in the Alps; the building of dams and water tunnels for high-pressure power plants is a classic area of Swiss engineering experimentation. Among the largest dams in the world, both in high valleys of the canton of Valais, are the Grand Dixence dam whose resistance relies on its weight, and the Mauvoisin dam whose resistance relies on the counterstress of its vault (*Fig. 19*).

Besides his contribution to modern bridge construction, Maillart made important advances in surface engineering, especially with his invention of mushroom-shaped vaults (1908) which acquired a new lightness when prestressed concrete recently came into use. The engineer Heinz Hossdorf, with the architect Florian Vischer, used plastics for his system of "mushrooms" in the interesting Pavilion of Economics at the 1964 Swiss National Exhibition (*Fig. 20*). In such examples engineering acquires a freshness and lightness of form seldom achieved even in those fields where much more architectural ambition is involved. The same can be said of technically less interesting structures such as the small manufacturing plant by Heinz Isler and Paul Wirz near Solothurn (*Fig. 21*).

The flourishing condition of Swiss industry and economics not only appears in engineering constructions and large industrial plants but also in administrative buildings which represent the economic power of the established industries and great insurance companies, Swiss as well as foreign, in the town centers. In general such administrative buildings, although often endowed with considerable architectural delicacy, remain behind their models in New York, Düsseldorf, or Milan. Furthermore, they usually show few features that can be considered "new directions," since the office layouts are dependent on international standards of measures and structural patterns which tend to limit the architectural possibilities of imaginative handling of proportion and urban setting. It has become a fashion in cities like Geneva, Lausanne, or Lugano to decorate such administrative buildings with opaque colored-glass facades which shine like mother-of-pearl.

There is one little-known administrative building that deserves particular attention. In the Fabrizia administration building in Bellinzona, Luigi Snozzi and Livio Vacchini have attempted to get away from the prevalent smooth curtain-wall facades which differ only in color and proportion. They have tried to give the office block an individual physiognomy by treating the surface structure somewhat like the body of a car with rounded edges at the corners and at the bottom (*Figs. 22–23*).

20. *Florian Vischer (architect) and Heinz Hossdorf (engineer): Pavilion of Economics, Swiss National Exposition, Lausanne, 1964.*

21. *Paul Wirz (architect) and Heinz Isler (engineer): Manufacturing plant, Recherswil, 1966.*

22. *Luigi Snozzi: Fabrizia administration building, Bellinzona, 1965.*

23. *Fabrizia administration building, section.*

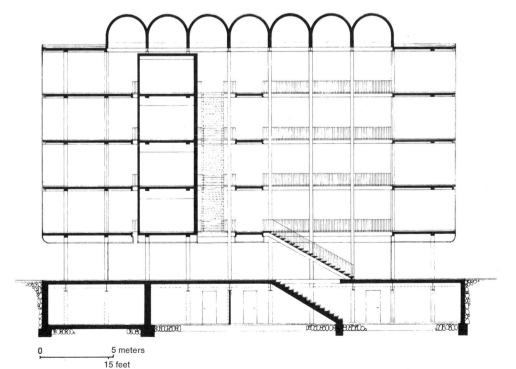

0   5 meters
    15 feet

24. Franz Füeg: Metal construction shop, Kleinlützel, 1958.

25. Metal construction shop, Kleinlützel, site plan and plan of first floor.

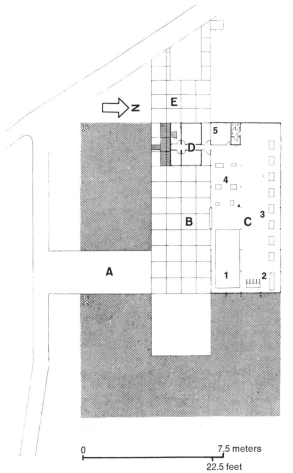

A. Entrance
B. Factory yard
C. Workshops
D. Office building
E. Parking area and
   entrance to office building

1. Storage
2. Bevelling and
   bending machines
3. Work benches
4. Metal- and woodwork
   machines
5. Foreman and tools

0   7,5 meters
                    22.5 feet

Industrial plants offer architects the most favorable field of experimentation, especially concerning variability and flexibility. They are determined by a far-sighted overall planning which is executed step by step according to the changing and partly unforeseeable needs of production. Rigorous as well as open modular systems are adopted here in a way which will not be without influence on other areas of building. While Franz Füeg's metal construction shop in Kleinlutzel near Basel (*Figs. 24–25*) expresses the demand for economic building with a remarkable purity and simplicity of form, Jean-Marc Lamuniere has incorporated a much more complicated task in a form which shows an almost luxurious handling of constructional detail and overall proportion (*Fig. 26*).

The factory at Bilten by Paul Waltenspuhl and Maurice Ziegler imaginatively shows how the demand for future extension and variability can be met in terms of vivid architectural and sculptural language (*Figs. 27–28*). The same is true for the factory they built at Näfels, in which the problem of overall lighting led to a particularly sensitive solution (*Figs. 29–30*). In their factory at Ecublens, Frei, Hunziker, and Hunziker emphasized illumination of the individual workshop place (*Fig. 31*). In Bert Allemann's and Hans Stunzi's factory and warehouse at Hochdorf, as in the former examples, the appropriate regulating of light has led to facades of unusual sculptural quality (*Figs. 32–33*).

26. Jean-Marc Lamunière: Industrial plant and warehouse, Renens, 1964.

27. *Paul Waltenspuhl and Maurice Ziegler: Factory, Bilten, 1963–1966.*

28. *Factory, Bilten, site plan.*

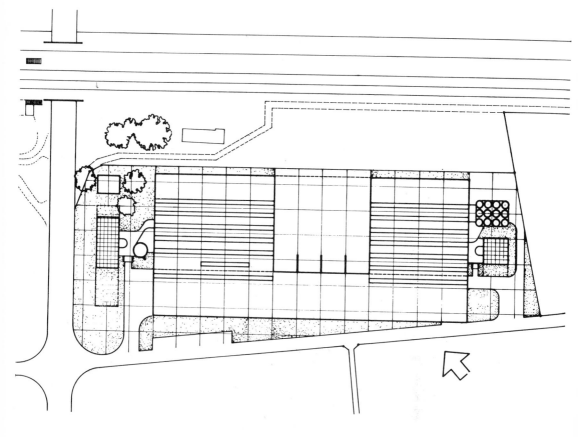

What has been said about engineering constructions also holds true for a building category that is prominent in Swiss architectural tradition: agricultural buildings and constructions. Although the vast regional variety of Swiss rustic architecture still represents a fascinating repertory of constructional skill and imagination, new forms must be found for the changing situation in agriculture today. Farming is turning into a thoroughly organized and specialized affair, especially in the Lowlands, as a growing number of individual farms are being integrated within cooperatives. New and positive architectural solutions have been realized mainly in such large-scale farming.

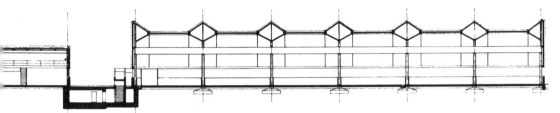

29. *Paul Waltenspuhl and Maurice Ziegler: Machine factory, Näfels, 1965, section.*

30. *Machine factory, Näfels, facade.*

31. Robert Frei, Christian and Jakob Hunziker: Factory, Ecublens, 1965.

32. Bert Allemann and Hans Stünzi: Factory and warehouse, Hochdorf, 1963–1964, detail of facade section.

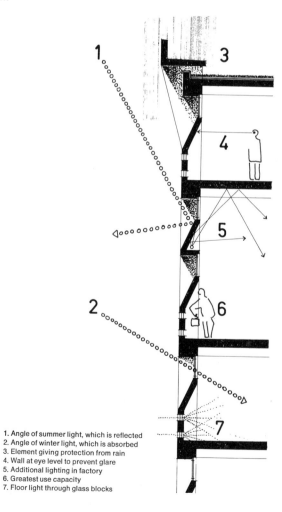

1. Angle of summer light, which is reflected
2. Angle of winter light, which is absorbed
3. Element giving protection from rain
4. Wall at eye level to prevent glare
5. Additional lighting in factory
6. Greatest use capacity
7. Floor light through glass blocks

In recent years soil enrichment and real estate mergers have given rise to the building of many new farming establishments which allow specialization as well as thorough mechanization. Since the separate establishments usually lie far apart, any far-reaching comprehensive planning and standardization, despite a number of serious attempts along these lines, encounters great difficulties. Thus the most convincing contributions to modern farm design are individual rather than typical solutions—quite in opposition to rustic architecture of the past. Their architectural approach comes very close to similar attempts in Denmark. One may also recall works done by Hugo Häring in the twenties and the thirties in Germany. Of course such elaborate designs as those by Jakob Zweifel (*Figs. 34–35*) or Heinz Hess (*Figs. 36–37*) are exceptions among many other, less inspired constructions. In general, the planning and construction of new farms is being simplified and rationalized by operational research, basic layout plans, and detailed financial and administrative calculation.

Housing

Terms such as "city" and "village" no longer imply definite human living patterns. The Swiss Midlands are gradually becoming a large industrial and habitational agglomeration. Today the centers of density are still the cities, but these high-density areas must be supplemented by new and better-equipped concentrations.

33. *Factory and warehouse, Hochdorf.*

With the growth of industrialization in the middle of the nineteenth century, the Swiss urban population multiplied within a few decades, after centuries of stability. Simultaneously a mutual migration into and out of the cities occurred. On the one hand the promising possibilities of the city attracted people from the country; on the other hand, wealthy town dwellers gradually retreated to the nearby countryside. The automobile caused an increased density of work and communication within the urban centers and at the same time gave rise to the scattering of habitation over an urban region. The population density in such an urban region is much lower than it was within the walls of former cities.

Thus, because of the rapid population increase, agricultural acreage and open areas in the Midlands are shrinking dangerously. It has been rightly said that the problem of housing in Switzerland lies not so much in the scarcity of land as in the construction of dwelling-types that are particularly land-consuming, such as row-houses.

The ideal of every Swiss is to have his own free-standing home. For many years public housing attempted to satisfy this desire psychologically, if not practically, by row dwellings and particularly "homely" appliances in the relatively small housing units (*Fig. 38*).

34. Jakob Zweifel: Agricultural plant, Bevaix, 1963–1964, ground plan.

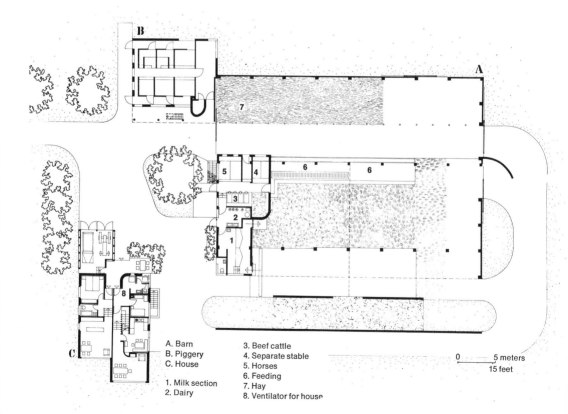

A. Barn
B. Piggery
C. House

1. Milk section
2. Dairy

3. Beef cattle
4. Separate stable
5. Horses
6. Feeding
7. Hay
8. Ventilator for house

0   5 meters
     15 feet

During the last ten years new building types have been proposed in an attempt to meet the specific problems of a country with limited building space. Le Corbusier's Unité d'habitation (1947–1952) in Marseille may have been a suggestive impulse toward the building of large slab structures such as the Tours de Carouge (*Figs. 39–40*) by Paul Waltenspuhl and collaborators. These large housing units near Geneva, which somewhat recall Corbusier's project for St. Dié, are an example of modern highrise slabs intelligently juxtaposed with valuable traditional environment. The towers, in whose neighborhood work is provided for 3,400 people, are fully integrated within the charming city of Carouge whose neoclassical buildings and regular plan are an extraordinary example of urban design in the last quarter of the eighteenth century.

By far the largest of these urban concentrations as well as the most refined in design is the enormous satellite city Cité du Lignon by Georges Addor, D. Juillard, Jacques Bolliger, and Louis Payot (*Figs. 41–42*). It consists of a bent slab which extends for over a kilometer and two brilliantly juxtaposed vertical slabs. The same architects had already built a "new city" of comparable size and elegance of design, the Cité du Meyrin, near Geneva. They seem to have been captivated by the grandiose character of their design and the supreme elegance of their shiny facades; in any case they have been much less concerned about the social quality of such an environment. In grand ensembles of this size, family life becomes very difficult, especially with children, and the dwellers behind these polished glass and aluminum facades live their lives in complete isolation. Thus social situations are created which are quite new in

35. Agricultural plant, Bevaix.

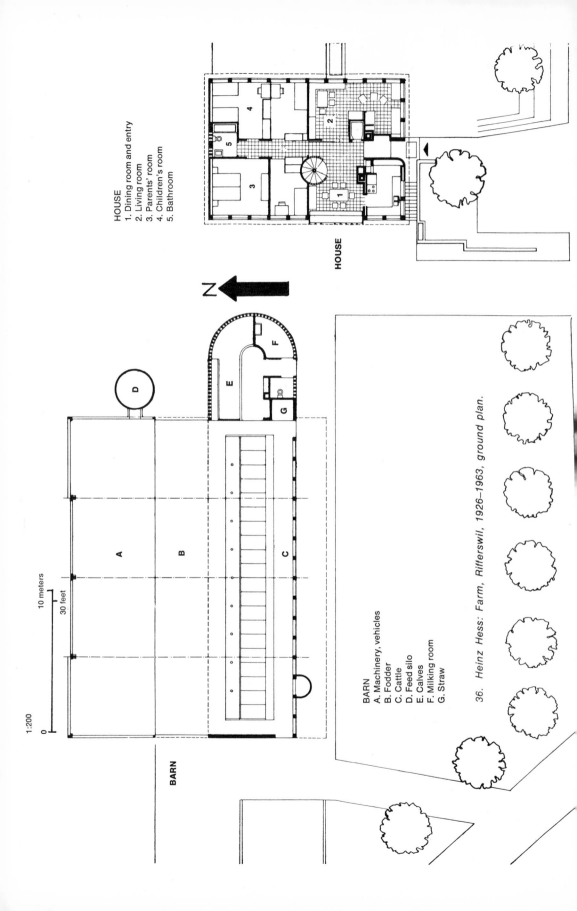

1:200

0   10 meters

30 feet

BARN

N

A

B

C

D

E

F

G

BARN
A. Machinery, vehicles
B. Fodder
C. Cattle
D. Feed silo
E. Calves
F. Milking room
G. Straw

HOUSE
1. Dining room and entry
2. Living room
3. Parents' room
4. Children's room
5. Bathroom

HOUSE

4

5

3

1

2

36. *Heinz Hess: Farm, Rifferswil, 1926–1963, ground plan.*

Switzerland and must be faced imaginatively. Eduard Helfer and Gret Reinhard have made an attempt along this line with their Gabelbach apartment blocks outside Bern (*Figs. 43–44*). These two enormous slabs, dramatically juxtaposed to the sharply broken terrain, are more lively than their forerunners in Geneva because of their more sculptural character created by the vivid and varied design of the facades, but especially because of easily accessible community facilities.

Other large housing blocks, less overwhelming in size and not always very imaginative in their ground plans, are interesting because of the remarkable quality of their architectural design and urban setting. Jean-Marc Lamunière has built the Tours de Lancy on a hillside near Geneva. Although unfortunately only two of the originally four planned towers have been built, these two structures already add considerably to the urban physiognomy of the city (*Figs. 45–46*). Rudolf and Esther Guyer have invested their impressive tower, Triemli, in the outskirts of Zurich, with dramatic but somehow morose sculptural power. The same architects have made, as we will see later, a very imaginative contribution to prefabrication in their military barracks at Bremgarten (*Figs. 110–111*).

In the field of housing the Zurich group of architects Fred Cramer, Werner Jaray, Claude Paillard. and Peter Leemann has made the most convincing advance in prefabricated building, with their Grüzefeld development in Winterthur (*Figs. 47–48*). Here prefabrication does not lead to mere uniformity but rather to a sculptural enrichment of architectural form. A very important idea—that of variability and of the single apartment as the nucleus of an urban environment—appears here in a suggestive architectural image, although this idea may not be entirely guaranteed technically and functionally. It is this idea that leads us to a few enterprises which, despite their comparatively small scale, one day may prove to be the most valuable contribution of Swiss architects toward a humanization of the urban and suburban habitat.

37. Farm, Rifferswil, north view.

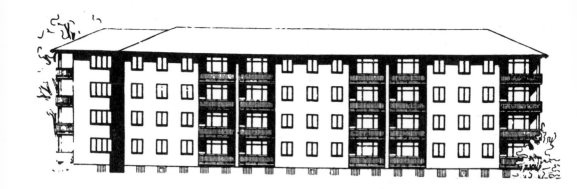

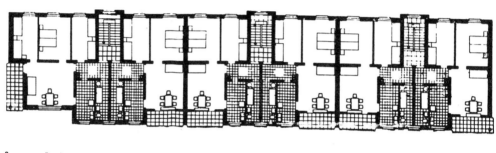

0   5 meters

38. Typical cooperative housing, around 1950.

39. Paul Waltenspuhl with Lucien Achinard, Georges Brera, Alfred Damay, Jean-Jacques Mégevand, and René Schwertz: Tours de Carouge, 1960. Old town of Carouge in foreground.

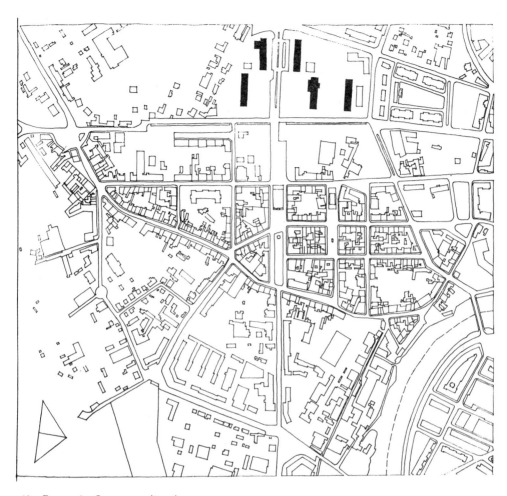

40. Tours de Carouge, site plan.

41. *Georges Addor, D. Juillard, Jacques Bolliger, Louis Payot: Cité du Lignon, 1962–1968, with Lake Geneva in background.*

42. *Cité du Lignon, site plan.*

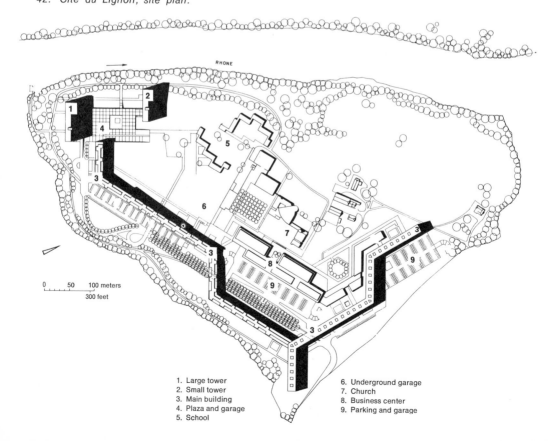

1. Large tower
2. Small tower
3. Main building
4. Plaza and garage
5. School

6. Underground garage
7. Church
8. Business center
9. Parking and garage

43. Haus and Gret Reinhard with Eduard Helfer: Gäbelbach blocks, Bern, 1965–1968.

44. Gäbelbach blocks, plan of typical floor.

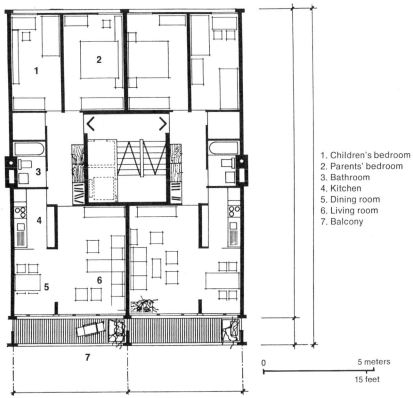

1. Children's bedroom
2. Parents' bedroom
3. Bathroom
4. Kitchen
5. Dining room
6. Living room
7. Balcony

0   5 meters

15 feet

A word may be added regarding the financial aspect of housing. Public housing accounts for only 2 percent of the dwellings built since 1960, and of the remainder only 10 percent has relied on the public assistance which is offered to low-rent housing projects. Since builders do not seem to favor this type of housing, the result is a definite lack of low-rent apartments. While low-rent apartments are hard to get, many new apartment houses cannot find enough tenants to occupy them from the start. In fact, the apartments built in Switzerland are the most expensive to build in the world. This is partly because of the 50,000 apartment units built annually only 7 percent are prefabricated.[14]

One may well ask why, when low-rent living facilities are so obviously needed, private citizens are equally ready to invest time and money in building single houses. Building seems to be one of the

45. Jean-Marc Lamunière: Tours de Lancy, Geneva, 1964.

most popular hobbies, after all—more popular at any rate than living in a building constructed by others! The future will have to provide a framework which encourages this individual building initiative and at the same time prevents total functional and visual chaos. For the moment, the extreme alternatives in modern housing are represented by the anonymous design of the Cité du Lignon in Geneva and the unplanned, individualistic "do-it-yourself" houses proposed by Frei, Hunziker, and Hunziker.

In their well-known Halen development near Bern, Atelier 5 and Niklaus Morgenthaler have spread out a "Unité d'habitation" with its characteristic collective services over a gentle slope (*Figs. 3, 49–50*). This inspiring arrangement of individual houses represents one of the most promising advances in rational land use. Situated in a wood clearing outside Bern, it suggests a method of concentrating

46. *Tours de Lancy, site plan. Only two towers (1) were built.*

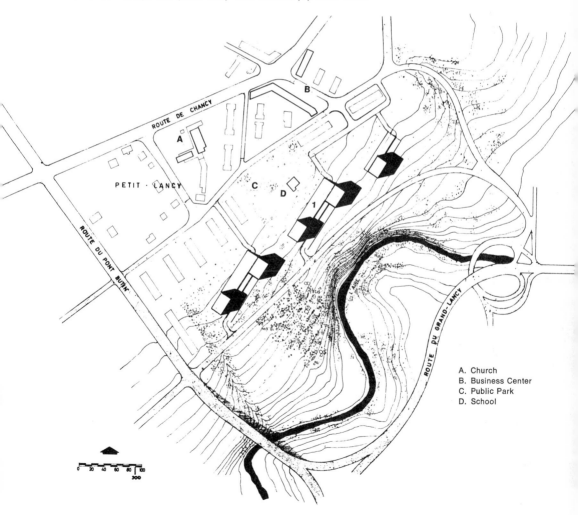

A. Church
B. Business Center
C. Public Park
D. School

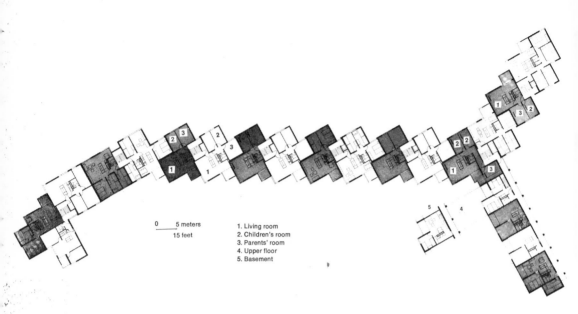

0   5 meters
    15 feet

1. Living room
2. Children's room
3. Parents' room
4. Upper floor
5. Basement

47. *Atelier Fred Cramer, Werner Jaray, and Claude Paillard (Claude Pailard and Peter Lee-mann, architects): Grüzefeld development, Winterthur, 1965–1968, plan of typical floor.*

48. *Gruzefeld development.*

49. *Atelier 5 and Niklaus Morgenthaler: Halen development, Bern, 1959–1961.*

50. *Halen development, site plan.*

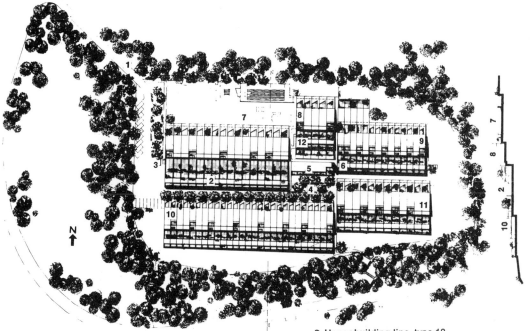

1. Driveway
2. Parking, under gardens
3. Gasoline station
4. Village center
5. Shop and restaurant
6. Heating, water, electricity
   facilities, under gardens
7. Swimming pool and deck
8. Upper building line, type 12
9. Upper building line, type 380
10. Under building line, type 12
11. Under building line, type 380
12. Studios

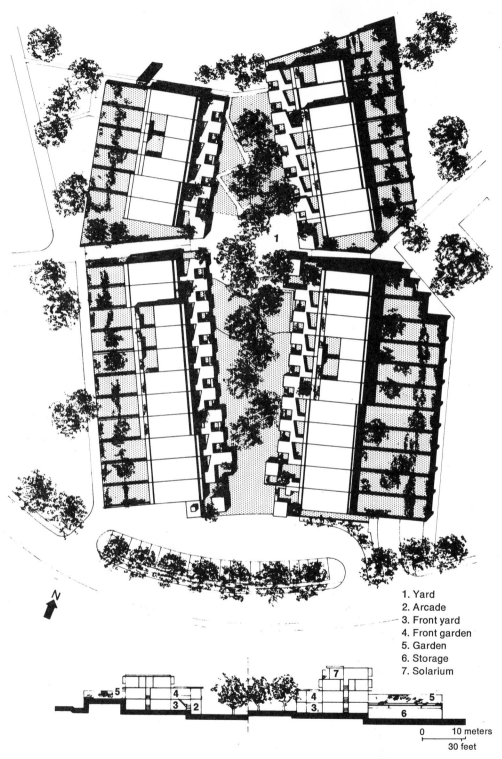

1. Yard
2. Arcade
3. Front yard
4. Front garden
5. Garden
6. Storage
7. Solarium

0   10 meters
     30 feet

51. *Atelier 5 and Niklaus Morgenthaler: Wertherberg housing development, near Münster, Germany, 1966–1968, site plan.*

individual dwellings in a comprehensive unit. The conception recalls late Corbusian projects such as the Roq et Rob settlement or the pilgrimage hostel of Sainte Baume, in southern France. The inhabitants of the seventy-nine houses, which are somewhat varied in plan and section, share the ownership of collective services such as the garage, heating plant, swimming pool, restaurant, the so-called "village square," and the narrow street within the compound.

In the Wertherberg housing development in Germany, Atelier 5 has considerably developed the Halen principle by a convincing arrangement of the service rooms of the single units (*Figs. 51–52*). The general design appears less systematic, thus encouraging a freer, more individual use of prefabricated elements. The concept of Halen is also carried further in a similar complex in Croydon, England, which is under construction (*Fig. 53*). On a smaller scale Thalmatt, near Bern, follows the same principle in a less rigid manner and with more individual variety.

The many hillsides and slopes in Switzerland have inspired a number of quite convincing terrace developments. This dwelling-type not only takes advantage of the many Midland slopes that are unsuitable for farming, but it offers a new quality of living environment

52. Wertherberg housing development.

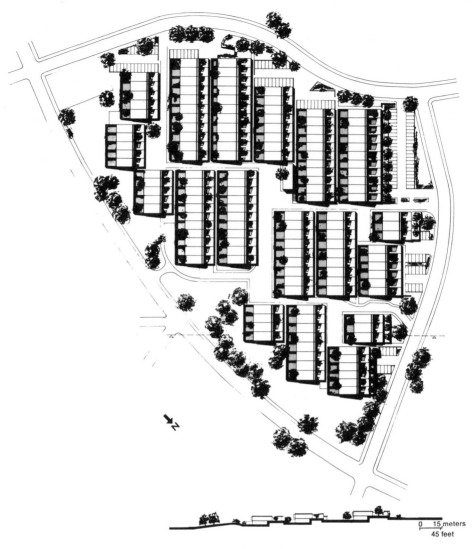

53. Atelier 5: Wates row houses, Croydon, England, 1967–1969, plan.

54. Fritz Stucky and Rudolf Meuli: Terrace apartments, Zug, 1958–1961.

and, most important of all, it leaves the precious space of the plain free for agriculture, industry, and traffic. One of the first terrace units in Switzerland was Wolfgang Muller's small kindergarten on the slope of the city fortress Munot in Schaffhausen (1932). In 1958–1961 Fritz Stucky and Rudolf Meuli built four structures whose apartments form an uphill terrace (*Fig. 54*). This building-type permitted the introduction of floor property (*Stockwerkeigentum*) in Swiss housing, since each floor lies partly on solid ground, if only for a few square meters. Previous to it, apartments could be rented only, not bought. A somewhat more elaborate quality of design was achieved

55. *Team 2000, Hans Ulrich Scherer and others (architects), and Metron group (execution): Terrace development, Umiken, 1963–1965.*

56. *Terrace development, Umiken, section.*

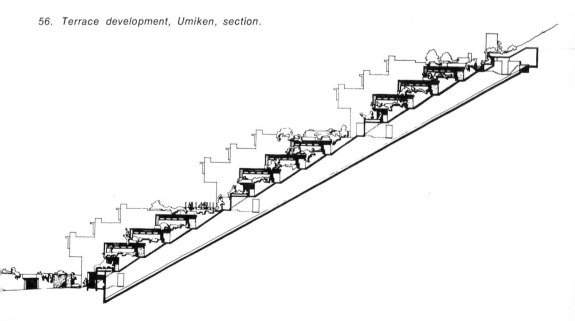

by Cramer, Jaray, and Paillard in their terrace development on the Eierbrechtstrasse in Witikon, near Zurich (1959).

More recently the idea of terrace developments was realized most successfully by Hans Ulrich Scherer, before his untimely death, and his collaborators, in Klingnau (1959–1963) and at the Brugger-berg, in Umiken, near Brugg (*Figs. 55–56*). The latter project is part of a large general plan, Brugg 2000, which includes office towers on the plain and terrace layouts served by sloping elevators. As yet only two units of this sloping settlement have been completed. How-ever, these two units, along with the Halen development, set a new standard for suburban housing in Switzerland, and although imitation may be dangerous, future projects can only profit by relying upon experiences gained here. Terrace developments are not bound to a particular formal approach: examples such as Otto Glaus's student dormitory in Chur (*Fig. 57*) or André Studer's terrace apartments at Visp (*Figs. 58–59*) prove that the idea can take quite different shapes and be successfully adapted to quite different purposes. Other ex-amples, of course, would demonstrate that this building-type does not in itself guarantee the embellishment of the landscape.

The back-to-nature movement of city dwellers is illustrated by the villas and weekend and vacation houses all over Switzerland, some of which are noteworthy for their high standard of design. The young Hans R. Bader from Solothurn has shown what a low-cost private home in a small town or village can look like (*Figs. 60–61*).

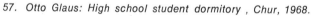

57. *Otto Glaus: High school student dormitory , Chur, 1968.*

58. André Studer: Terrace apartments, Visp, 1964–1967.

59. Terrace apartments, Visp, section.

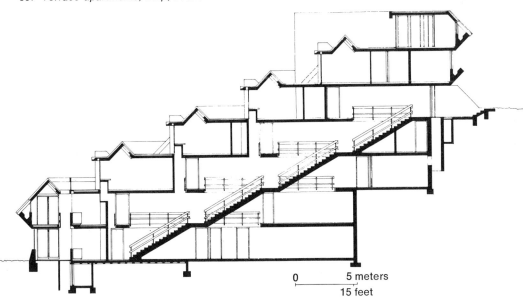

0 5 meters
15 feet

60. Hans R. Bader: Low-cost private home, Rüttenen, 1962–1963.

61. Private home, Rüttenen, plan.

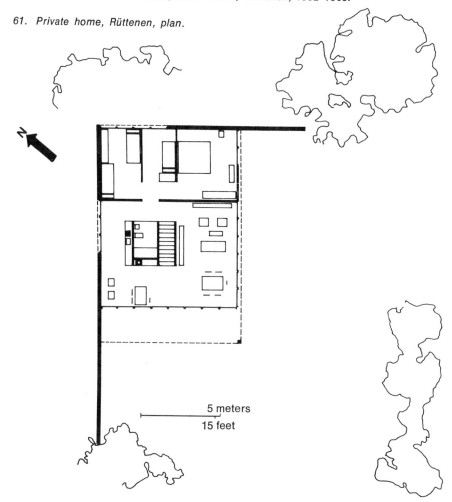

5 meters
15 feet

Ulrich Low and Theodor Manz have arranged a large number of L-shaped houses in carpet settlements in the outskirts of Basel (*Figs. 62–63*). These settlements, somehow more rigid than comparable enterprises of Jorn Utzon in Denmark, approach a type of housing proposed by José Luis Sert for American suburbs, although they do not include patios in the original sense of the word. In Basel their important forerunners are in Hannes Meyer's and Hans Bernoullis' settlements of the twenties.

Although it is not very encouraging to see how private villas today are scattered about Swiss towns and villages, it is in this area that architects present particularly elaborate formal realizations. Peppo Brivio's cubic approach in his small Casa Corinna near Chiasso (*Figs. 64–65*) is a much clearer and more coherent statement than his large apartment blocks in Lugano. Yet we may also draw attention to a work that is notable precisely for its lack of architectural pretension: Luigi Snozzi's Casa Snider in Verscio, near Locarno (*Figs. 66–67*). It is imaginatively integrated in its rustic surroundings, with which its pure forms harmonize excellently.

In the Ticino region, one of the main Swiss vacation resorts, tourism creates the most visible architectural complications and calls for a conscious solution. Throughout the nineteenth century the first phase of tourism brought huge resort hotels into the Swiss landscape. Today the changed characteristics of tourism have altered its architectural appearance. One could say that the second phase is less relevant architecturally, for it has turned many beautiful areas into camping sites with gaudy tents and caravans. But architects as well as highway planners must cope with mass tourism.

71

62. *Ulrich Löw and Theodor Manz: Carpet settlement, Reinach, 1959–1961.*

63. *Ulrich Löw and Theodor Manz: Carpet settlements, Reinach and Binningen, plans.*

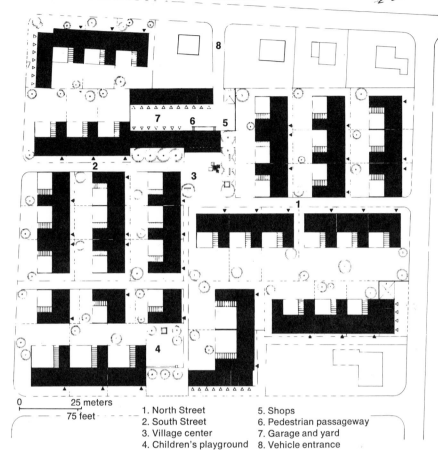

0	25 meters
	75 feet

1. North Street   5. Shops
2. South Street   6. Pedestrian passageway
3. Village center   7. Garage and yard
4. Children's playground 8. Vehicle entrance

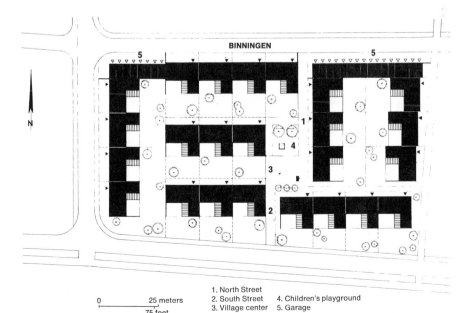

BINNINGEN

0	25 meters
	75 feet

1. North Street
2. South Street   4. Children's playground
3. Village center   5. Garage

73

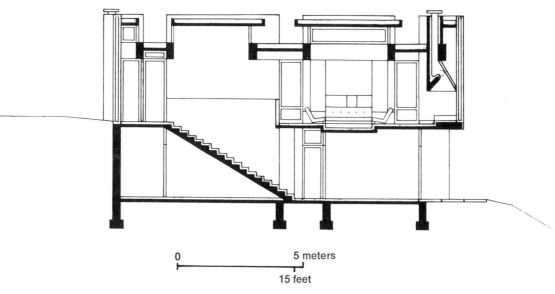

```
0                    5 meters
├──────────────────────┤
              15 feet
```

64. Peppo Brivio: Casa Corinna, Morbio Superiore, near Chiasso, 1962–1963, section.

65. Casa Corinna.

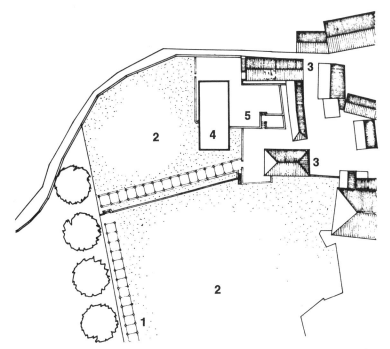

1. Main entrance
2. Garden
3. Old buildings
4. New building
5. Yard

66. *Luigi Snozzi: Casa Snider, Verscio, 1965, site plan.*

67. *Casa Snider.*

When, one day, jets will bring 500 tourists to Zurich on one flight, where will the visitors stay overnight if the airport hotel does not offer the necessary facilities? Indeed, there are very few far-sighted ideas about coping with such future invasions.

In the meantime Manuel Pauli has built a series of mushroom-like weekend or vacation houses above Locarno (*Figs. 68–69*), and André Studer proposes a similar though somewhat more futuristic type of vacation center north of Lucerne (*Figs. 70–71*). He has envisaged a self-contained, village-like settlement in the form of

68. Manuel Pauli: "Tre Tetti" group of vacation houses, Locarno-Monti, 1964–1965, ground plans and section.

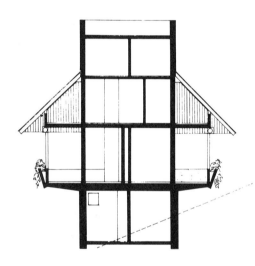

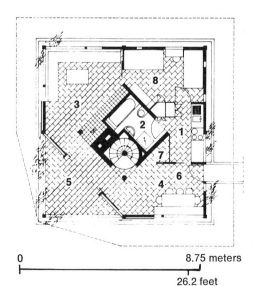

1. Kitchen
2. Bathroom
3. Living room
4. Dining room
5. Balcony
6. Entry
7. Cloakroom
8. Rooms
9. Heating
10. Cellar

0   8.75 meters

26.2 feet

cost-saving, prefabricated housing cells which hang in a suspension system containing supply facilities. Whether his project will be executed, however, is not certain.

The problems of tourism and vacation imply an even more general problem of modern civilization: leisure. Are we entering a time of extensive leisure? The architects Frei, Hunziker, and Hunziker apparently think so; they are trying to reestablish building as a main "do-it-yourself" activity. In the private houses at Puplinge and Gland (*Figs. 72–74*) they have sought to involve the owners and workmen

69. Tre Tetti.

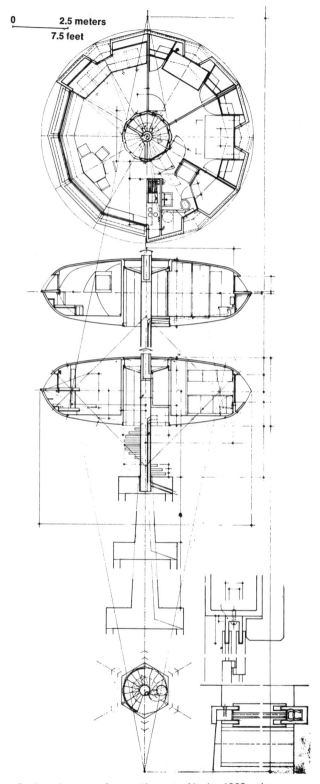

0   2.5 meters
    7.5 feet

70. *Andre Studer: Project for vacation settlement, Altwis, 1968, plan.*

creatively in the building process. Under the architects' guidance, imagination and play instinct are given full scope. A sort of psychology of the intimate factors of the building process could result from such experiments; for, of course, this is not "architecture" in any conventional sense of the word. Although the architects are not offering a pertinent answer to our present building problems they are stating a point which should not be overlooked. At a time when not only architectural science fiction but also much current building relies on a concept of man's servitude to technology, these architects are raising the question of whether we should indeed get involved with technology to that extent.

71. *Vacation settlement, Altwis, model.*

72. *Robert Frei, Christian and Jakob Hunziker: House, Gland, 1959–1962.*

73. *Robert Frei, Christian and Jakob Hunziker: House, Puplinge, 1965.*

Community Buildings

Today a new church, such as the Catholic church at Meggen (*Figs. 122–123*), can more closely resemble a factory such as the large printing plant at Renens (*Fig. 26*), than another church, for instance the Catholic College church at Sarnen (*Figs. 118–119*). A basic typological difference among the conventional building categories is no longer perceptible. The only difference now lies in the emotional approach. Naturally the treatment of space in a church will be more refined, differentiated, and subtle than in, for example, a factory or a garage.

With community buildings the problem of monumentality arises. Formerly the monumentality of town halls, churches, and schools consisted mainly in evoking memories of the past. Today monumentality depends above all on the degree of explicit articulation and sculptural enhancement of a building's structural aspects and spatial implications. Monumental ambition is, of course, exercised particularly on buildings where people congregate: theaters, churches, and, to a certain extent, schools. Thus without doubt such community buildings display the highest artistic refinement of contemporary Swiss architecture. One must take into account, however, that it is precisely this refinement that gives so many of these buildings their somewhat effeminate and fashionable appearance. The emphasis on the handling of interior space has had interesting

74. House, Puplinge, scheme.

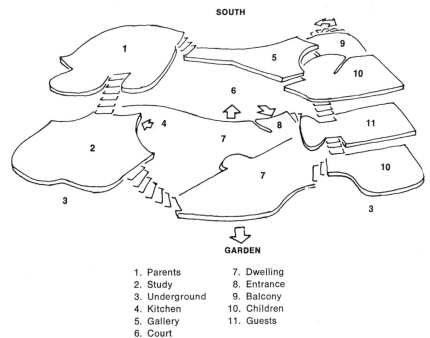

SOUTH

GARDEN

1. Parents
2. Study
3. Underground
4. Kitchen
5. Gallery
6. Court
7. Dwelling
8. Entrance
9. Balcony
10. Children
11. Guests

results. Spatial sequences, the enhancement and limitation of space, the gradation, torsion, and interpenetration of spaces are expressed with particular aptitude in some recent churches (*Figs. 116–121*). Experiments with the classical sobriety of mere volumetric cubes are also underway (*Figs. 122–123*).

While in postwar Germany new luxurious theaters became a sort of cultural status symbol of the new affluent society, in Switzerland only one new theater has been constructed which is comparable to the large theater and opera houses in Germany: the recently opened theater of St. Gallen by Cramer, Jaray, and Paillard (*Figs. 75–76*). In Zurich there is some hope that Jørn Utzon will build the new *Schauspielhaus* for which he won the competition in 1966. On

75. *Atelier Fred Cramer, Werner Jaray, and Claude Paillard (Claude Paillard and H. J. Gugler, architects): Theater, St. Gallen, 1964–1968.*

the other hand, officials in Zurich are about to sacrifice the Zurich Opera House, an excellent example of late-nineteenth-century theater architecture, for a modern design whose architectural quality lies far behind its ambition.

There is an extraordinary early example of a modern theater in Switzerland. The Theatre du Jorat at Mezieres, by Paillard and Charles (1907–1908), ten miles north of Lausanne, is halfway between a rustic barn and a traditional theater (*Figs. 77–78*). Its antithesis is Rudolf Steiner's Goetheanum at Dornach, the world center of anthroposophy (rebuilt 1925–1928), whose amorphous concrete building mass is a remarkable ancestor of many recent architectural developments (*Fig. 79*).

76. Theater, St. Gallen, ground plan.

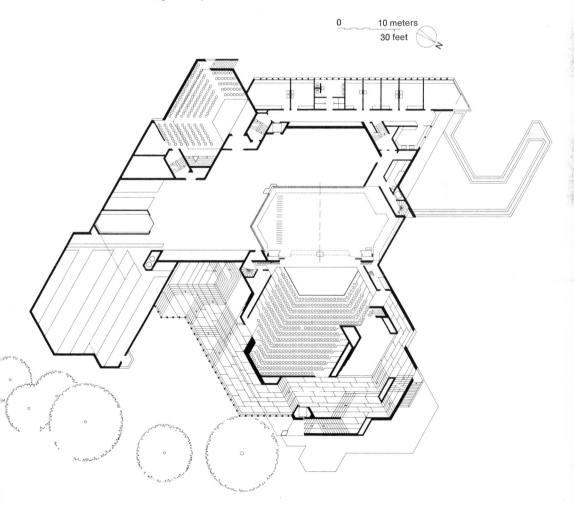

77. *Paillard and Charles: Théâtre du Jorat, Mézières, 1907–1908, exterior.*

78. *Théâtre du Jorat, interior.*

In 1954 Ernst Gisel built a community center at Grenchen, north of Bern (*Fig. 8*), comparable to Alvar Aalto's Säynätsalo community center (1951–1952). This remarkable building, articulated by sharply contrasting volumes, contains an auditorium and, in a lateral wing, a restaurant and a hotel. In the nearby city of Biel, Max Schlup has recently completed a much more extensive multipurpose community center, in which an indoor swimming pool, spacious concert hall, and a restaurant are accommodated under one enormous suspension roof (*Figs. 80–81*). Although much larger in scale and broader in function, this structure still lacks the unity of design which marks Gisel's park theater.

Such multipurpose community centers are still few in number, but they represent the growing demand for buildings which not only exhibit the community spirit of their builders but, more important, offer the space necessary for a variety of social activities. In fact, schools and churches are opening their doors to many community functions such as recreation, adult education, and political forums; thus they are becoming more integrated into community life. This

79. *Rudolf Steiner: Goetheanum, Dornach, rebuilt 1925–1928.*

trend may be exemplified by Walter M. Forderer's project of an
ecclesiastical community center in Heremence, near Sion (*Figs. 116–
117*). But conceiving community buildings for several different purposes is not a recent development. During school vacations, Swiss
Army troops are often quartered in empty school buildings. The vacation center at Fiesch by Paul Morisod, Jean Kyburz, and Edouard
Furrer was actually designed as a military hospital (*Figs. 82–83*).

Since responsibility for elementary education is entirely a local
matter in Switzerland, Swiss school planning is as uncoordinated and
almost as conservative as Swiss education systems themselves. Yet
community school building, with church architecture, is the main
source of community pride. This was already true in the last century,
when the classic type of Swiss school was created (*Fig. 84*)—a

80. *Max Schlup: Community center, with indoor swimming pool, Biel, 1961–1966, section.*

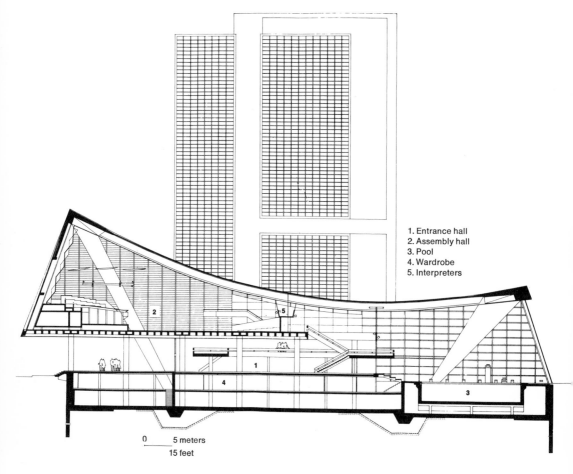

1. Entrance hall
2. Assembly hall
3. Pool
4. Wardrobe
5. Interpreters

0   5 meters
15 feet

type that to a certain extent reappears in the clear distinction of serving and served spaces in Hans R. Bader's recent projects (*Fig. 86*)—and the most original proposals for school furniture were advanced (*Fig. 85*).

The interior structure of schools has undergone little change in the last twenty years. Replacing oblong by square classrooms of about 80 square meters has become a common practice. More recently "group rooms," niches, or adjacent rooms have been added to the classrooms. New methods of cooperation among groups of pupils, as well as new technical methods, are being envisaged for the future. In view of this more differentiated teaching, the Zurich architect Roland Gross, who is the expert among young Swiss architects in the field of modern educational theory, has proposed the combination of two-class units with one group room (*Fig. 87*).

81. *Community center, Biel.*

82. *Paul Morisod, Jean Kyburz, and Edouard Furrer: Vacation center, Fiesch, 1966–1968.*

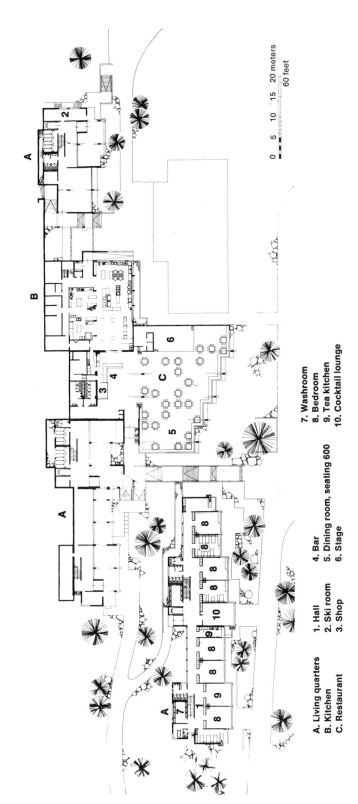

A. Living quarters
B. Kitchen
C. Restaurant

1. Hall
2. Ski room
3. Shop

4. Bar
5. Dining room, seating 600
6. Stage

7. **Washroom**
8. **Bedroom**
9. **Tea kitchen**
10. **Cocktail lounge**

0   5   10   15   20 meters
                    60 feet

83. *Vacation center, Fiesch, ground plan of one part.*

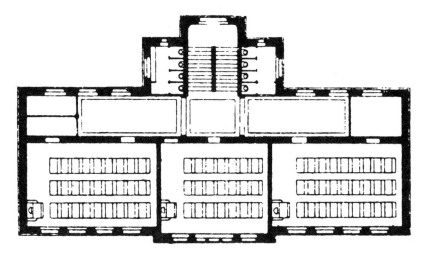

84. *Typical late-nineteenth-century Swiss school, plan.*

85. *J. Grob (schoolteacher, Zurich): Sitting machine, about 1900.*

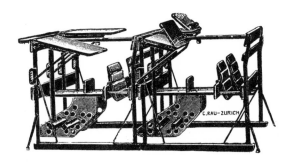

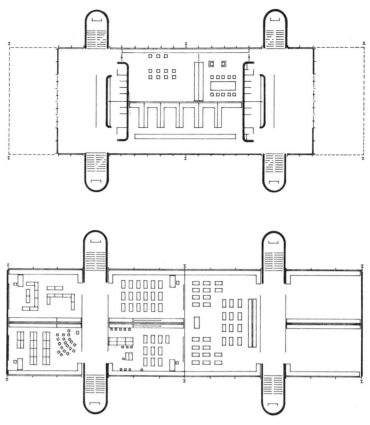

86. *Hans R. Bader: First-place competition project for a new school, Brüel, 1968, ground floor and second floor.*

87. *Roland Gross, Hans Escher, and Robert Weilenmann: Primary and secondary school, Zurich-Affoltern, 1959. Foreground, primary class unit. Background, secondary school tower.*

Education is demanding building flexibility. But few examples exist, except for the Frauenfeld high school by Alfons Barth and Hans Zaugg (1966–1968), in which an almost total variability of interior space distribution leads to an almost equally total renunciation of architectural form. In recent competitions Hans R. Bader and Luigi Snozzi have presented the most interesting contributions to this problem (*Figs. 13, 86*). In their designs only the basic serving appliances (such as water, electricity, gas) and the serving spaces of the stairs are fixed, and within this framework all manner of future extensions and changes in usage are made possible in a way that recalls design practices in industrial buildings. Bruno and Fritz Haller's technical high school in Windisch is also focused on flexibility; at the same time it achieves an unusual, sophisticated elegance of design (*Figs. 88–89*). Another example along the same lines is the Säli School in Olten by Alfons Barth and Hans Zaugg (*Figs. 90–91*).

Most of the more recent schools, however, rely on less advanced methods of planning and building. Frédéric Brugger's large complex "de L'Elysée" in Lausanne, containing a secondary school and an art school, somewhat echoes the well-known Freudenberg High School in Zurich by Jacques Schader (1956–1960). But while the latter is a building complex of marked monumental ambition, "de L'Elysée" is as human in its character as it is cultivated and imaginative in its design (*Figs. 92–93*).

Ernst Gisel, whose Letzi secondary school in Zurich (1955–1956) is still a landmark of modern school architecture, recently built a school in Engelberg (*Figs. 94–95*). Its interest lies more in its sculptural qualities than in its organization: the sharply articulated, massive reinforced concrete structure seems to answer the rugged forms of the surrounding alpine rocks.

88. *Bruno and Fritz Haller: Technical high school, Windisch, 1964–1966.*

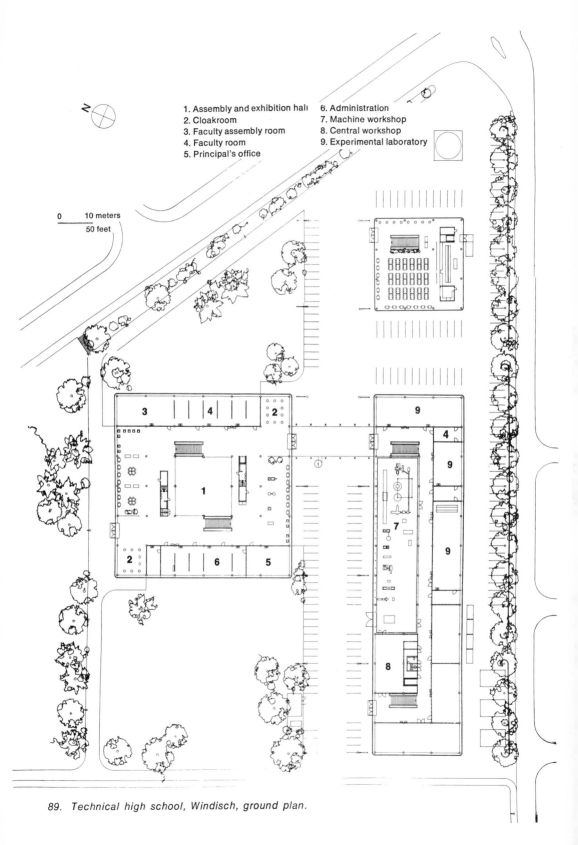

N

1. Assembly and exhibition hall
2. Cloakroom
3. Faculty assembly room
4. Faculty room
5. Principal's office

6. Administration
7. Machine workshop
8. Central workshop
9. Experimental laboratory

0   10 meters
     50 feet

89. *Technical high school, Windisch, ground plan.*

90. *Alfons Barth and Hans Zaugg: Säli school, Olten, 1964–1968.*

91. *Säli school, site plan.*

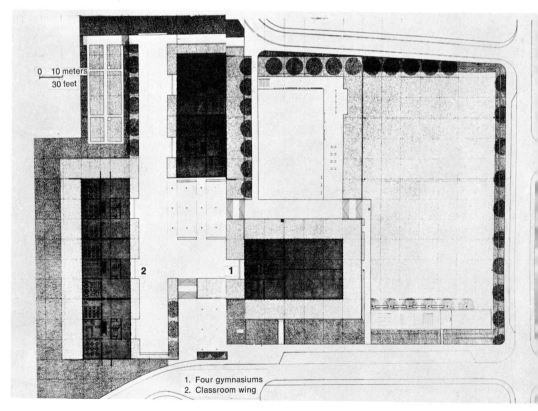

0   10 meters
30 feet

2   1

1. Four gymnasiums
2. Classroom wing

In 1938–1939 Hermann Baur built the Bruderholz school in Basel, whose pavilion layout has become very influential in Swiss school design. Recently the idea of a pavilion school has been reformulated in a more specific way. With the isolation of separate class units as cubic cells with interspaces for open air instruction, schools have been increasingly transformed into free agglomerations of cellular units. In Geneva Georges Candilis and Arthur Bugna realized this idea in their small French School (*Figs. 96–97*), and in an open landscape Alfons Barth and Hans Zaugg revived this theme in their much larger Scheibenschachen school-complex in Aarau (1962–1964). Perhaps the most imaginative achievements are those of Dolf Schnebli in his junior high school at Locarno with its original skylight system (*Figs. 98–99*), and in his Bunzmatt school and bathing establishment at Wohlen (*Figs. 100–101*). These realizations may be regarded as experimental prototypes for a future urban esthetic in the direction of group form, as presented for example in Moshe Safdie's Habitat 67 in Montreal. On the other hand, the demand for economy, flexibility, and normalization leads back to more compact solutions. The most advanced statements of these aims are found in kindergarten design, such as the Metron group's kindergarten element system which has recently been applied in Niederlenz (*Figs. 102–103*).

92. *Frederic Brugger: "De l'Elysée" secondary and art school, Lausanne, 1961–1964, entrance hall.*

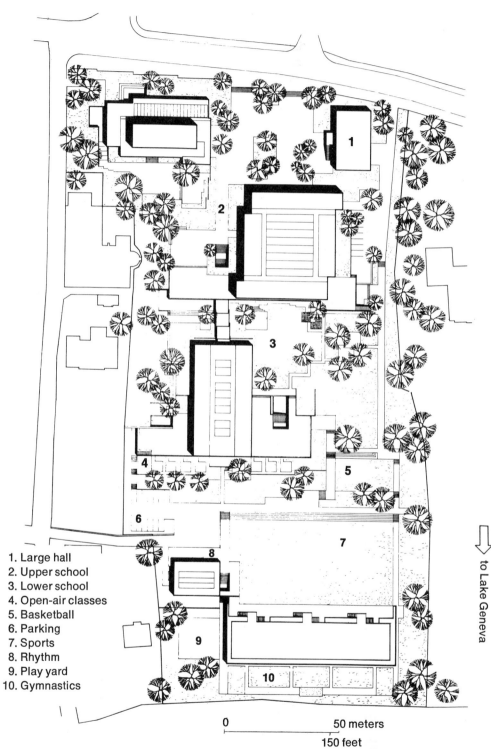

1. Large hall
2. Upper school
3. Lower school
4. Open-air classes
5. Basketball
6. Parking
7. Sports
8. Rhythm
9. Play yard
10. Gymnastics

to Lake Geneva

| 0 | 50 meters |

150 feet

93. *"De l'Elysée" secondary and art school, site plan.*

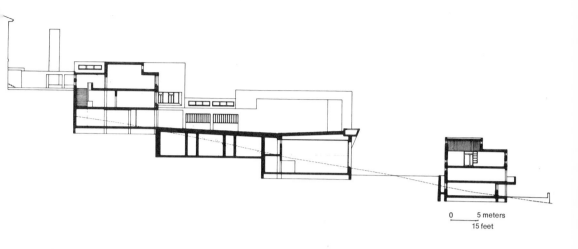

94. *Ernst Gisel: School, Engelberg, 1965–1967, section.*

95. *School, Engelberg.*

96. *Georges Candilis and Arthur Bugna: French School, Geneva, 1964.*

97. *French School.*

98. Dolf Schnebli: Junior high school, Locarno, 1963.

99. Junior high school, Locarno, section of classroom units.

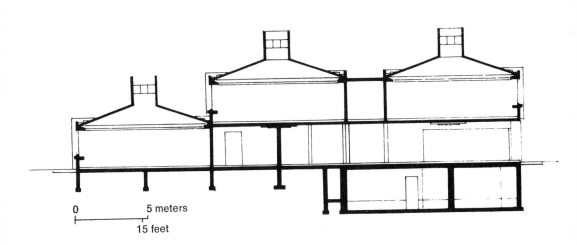

0   5 meters

15 feet

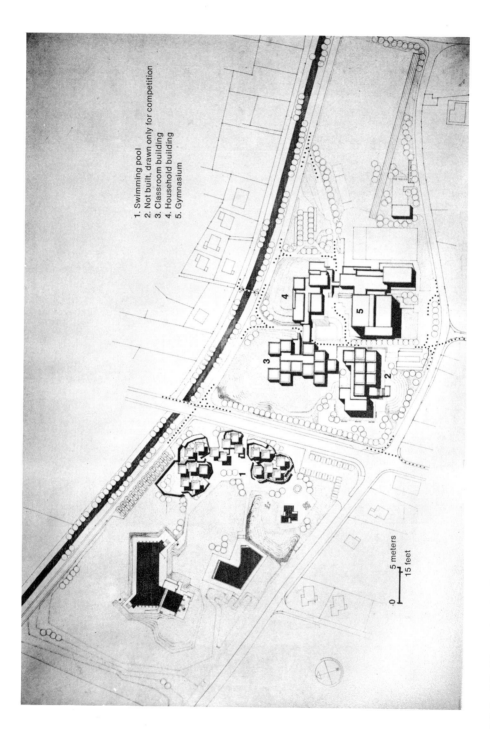

1. Swimming pool
2. Not built, drawn only for competition
3. Classroom building
4. Household building
5. Gymnasium

100. Dolf Schnebli: Bünzmatt school and bathing establishment, Wohlen, 1966, site plan.

0   5 meters
15 feet

101. *Bünzmatt school and bathing establishment, court.*

102. *Metron group: Kindergarten, Niederlenz, 1963.*

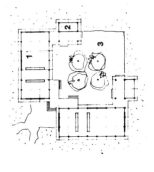

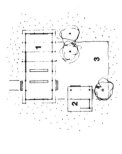

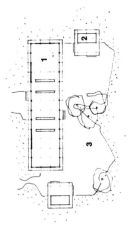

A. Simple school unit
B. Double school unit

1. Kindergarten
2. Outside tool shop
3. Yard

103. Metron group: Various adaptions of the kindergarten-element system.

Leisure and recreation are as great a problem in the larger Swiss towns as in other countries. Exemplary planning has created recreation centers for young people in many districts in Zurich. The centers contain large workshops, libraries, auditoriums for theatrical and musical performances, and sports facilities. Many youths find in them a counterbalance to the emptiness of their family lives. The future will show whether such facilities can interest young people in community life and whether they can counteract the television mania. Much will depend on how the centers are organized and managed. The youth of Zurich has for many years demanded an "autonomous youth center," as yet without success.

Hans Litz and Fritz Schwarz gave their Heuried recreation center in Zurich (*Figs. 104–105*) the shape of a model suburban community center. Up to now, however, it remains questionable whether the architects' ideals correspond with the ideals of those for whom the center has been designed; only the remarkable building playground is a complete success. Among new indoor swimming pools, Ernst Gisel's contribution in Davos (*Figs. 106–107*) is noteworthy for its organization and subtle design.

In Switzerland, the country of Pestalozzi, there is always a strong tendency to make leisure fruitful in terms of education. Seldom has this idea been realized with such charm as in Wolfgang Behles' Children's Zoo in Rapperswil near Zurich (*Figs. 108–109*), a somewhat exotic architectural environment for the elephants, the gnus, the rhinoceroses, and the birds of the Swiss National Circus, the *Zirkus Knie*.

Like the building of schools, the building of military barracks is evolving in a direction far from the nineteenth-century ideal of representative school- or military-palaces, in order to meet the needs of the increasingly specialized Swiss militia. For the new barracks at Bremgarten, Rudolf and Esther Guyer developed a very elaborate system of prefabricated elements, which gives the building complex a rigid and muscular appearance (*Figs. 110–111*). The military base at Bremgarten by the same architects (*Figs. 112–113*) shares its temporary character and its transportability with the kindergarten mentioned above.

For centuries the most representative community buildings in Europe have been churches. Although this is still somewhat the case, church building today, Catholic or Protestant, has become rather the problem child of modern architecture. It is true that Swiss architects have built many dignified churches since the thirties. In recent years the emotional impact of the task has had very positive, but also very ambiguous results.

The abandonment of the traditional concept of a church as well as the loosening of liturgical conventions have created a demand

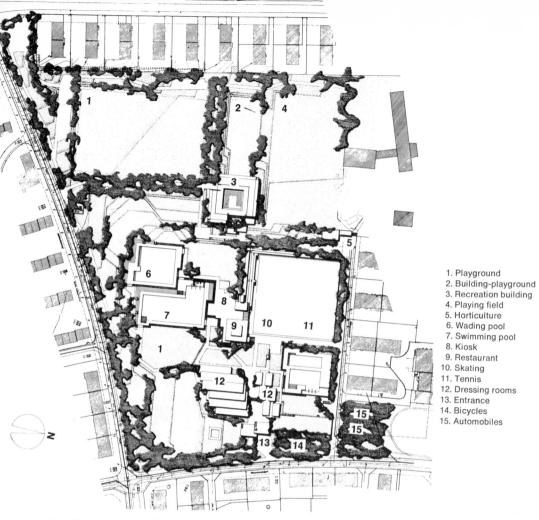

1. Playground
2. Building-playground
3. Recreation building
4. Playing field
5. Horticulture
6. Wading pool
7. Swimming pool
8. Kiosk
9. Restaurant
10. Skating
11. Tennis
12. Dressing rooms
13. Entrance
14. Bicycles
15. Automobiles

104. *Hans Litz and Fritz Schwarz: Heuried recreation center, Zurich-Wiedikon, 1962–1965, site plan.*

105. *Heuried recreation center, children's building playground.*

106. *Ernst Gisel: Indoor swimming pool, Davos, 1964–1965.*

107. *Indoor swimming pool, Davos, ground floor with pool and restaurant.*

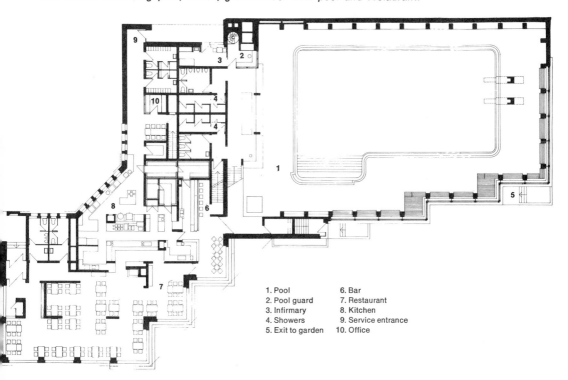

1. Pool
2. Pool guard
3. Infirmary
4. Showers
5. Exit to garden

6. Bar
7. Restaurant
8. Kitchen
9. Service entrance
10. Office

for new architectural forms. Thus church architecture has become a large field of architectural experimentation and often doubtful artistic virtuosity. Of course, the freeing of Swiss church architecture from its traditional forms would have occurred even less dramatically and less rapidly had not Le Corbusier, some fifty miles northwest of the Swiss border, built his chapel of Notre-Dame-du-Haut at Ronchamp (1950–1955), which in Switzerland has become one of the most admired and yet most misunderstood landmarks of modern architecture.

During the last ten years more new churches have been built in Switzerland than during the preceding fifty years. At the same time statistics clearly show that church attendance is persistently dwindling. Yet the building of churches continues. This can be explained partly by the fact that church taxes are collected by the state; thus the financial situation of a church depends on the number of tax-paying citizens in its congregation rather than on their personal engagement.

Religious circles more and more openly express the conviction that the current boom in church building has more to do with the social mechanisms of present society than with the demands of a church which in today's world is no longer culturally dominant. In fact, it has become questionable whether "the sacral as the political visualization of the religious,"[15] which has been the essence of traditional European religious culture, still fits into current social patterns. Thus the church in the "post-sacral" epoch retreats more and more into diaspora and, instead of upholding its historical commanding position in society, tries to become a part of secular community life and all its social activities.

108. *Wolfgang Behles: Children's Zoo, Rapperswil, 1961–1962.*

109. *Children's Zoo, ground floor, exotic animals stable.*

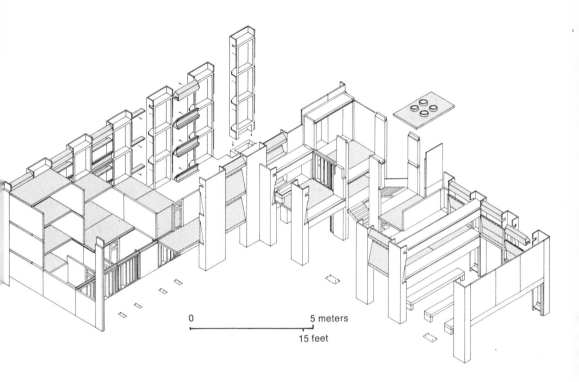

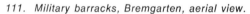

0   5 meters

15 feet

110. *Rudolf and Esther Guyer, and Manuel Pauli: Military barracks, Bremgarten, 1965–1968, isometric drawing of building sector with prefabricated elements.*

111. *Military barracks, Bremgarten, aerial view.*

112. *Rudolf and Esther Guyer: Military base, Bremgarten, 1965–1968.*

113. *Military base, Bremgarten, ground plan.*

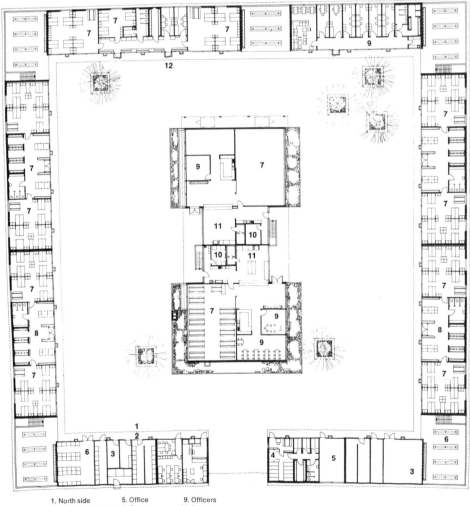

1. North side
2. Covered corridor
3. Utensils
4. Guard
5. Office
6. Camp
7. Soldiers
8. Washrooms
9. Officers
10. Storage
11. Kitchen
12. South side

The young Basel architect Rainer Senn makes claims for a church architecture in the spirit of poverty (*Figs. 114–115*). Some of his works indicate that a true renovation of church architecture in this spirit seems possible, as it was in the churches of the orders of mendicant friars in the late Middle Ages. In contrast to this approach, Walter M. Förderer is instrumenting his multifaceted ecclesiastical community centers with a bombastic architectural orchestration. He aims to bring the altar closer to the everyday living environment of the people. His church at Hérémence can also be used as a theater, concert hall, or discussion forum, and the tower contains living quarters (*Figs. 116–117*).

In the meantime churches in the traditional sense of the word continue to be built. While architects try to cope with the new liturgical requirements, the need for churches to meet specific liturgical functions is often overestimated. As with schools, the recent developments in church building are primarily architectural and formal rather than symbolic or theological. Thus they are far more symptomatic of the current state of architecture than that of religious culture in Switzerland. Three recent churches may illustrate the wide range of architectural idioms mastered by Swiss architects; never has the range of possibilities between sculptural expressionism and crystalline purism been so comparatively wide.

114. *Rainer Senn: Poor people's church, near Nizza, southern France (no longer standing).*

The church of the Catholic College in Sarnen by Joachim Naef and Ernst and Gottlieb Studer (*Figs. 118–119*) is related to Baroque architecture, which found particularly fertile ground in central Switzerland in the seventeenth and eighteenth centuries. Its sculptured volume reflects precisely the strongly differentiated interior spaces. A comparable result, although formally more rigid, has been achieved by Hanns Brütsch in his Catholic church at Buchs (*Figs. 120–121*).

In contrast, Franz Fueg followed the ideal of classical purity of form in his Catholic church at Meggen (*Figs. 122–123*). Füeg has

115. Rainer Senn: Church, Villejuif, near Paris, 1966.

been influenced by Angelo Mangiarotti's and Bruno Morassutti's parish church in Baranzate, an industrial suburb of Milan (1957–58). While in Mangiarotti's beautiful church the walls consist of inexpensive neutral industrial glasses, in Fueg's church the Greek alabaster of the walls plunges the interior in a stormy twilight. The result may not be entirely satisfactory. Nevertheless it represents a serious attempt at escaping the present trend toward mere individualistic and experimental church architecture. The future will show whether this concept is reactionary or whether it carries within itself the germ of developments to come.

116. *Walter M. Forderer; Ecclesiastical community center, Heremence, under construction, model of interior.*

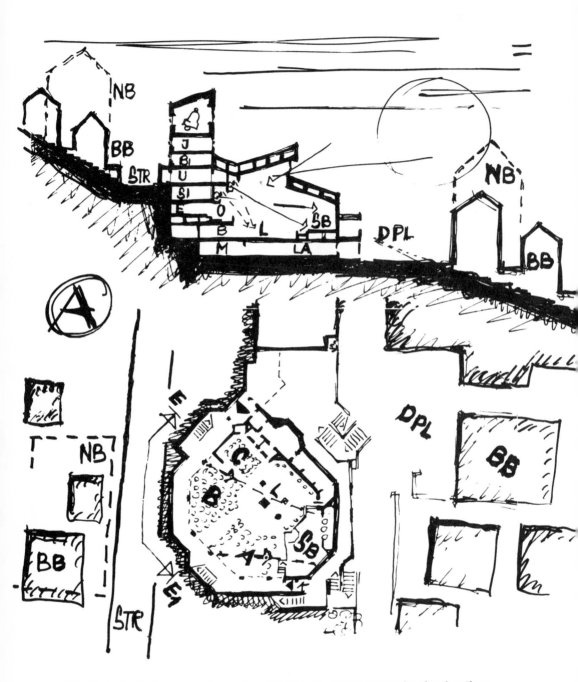

117. Ecclesiastical community center, Hérémence, sketch of overlapping functions.

118. *Joachim Naef, Ernst and Gottlieb Studer: Church of the Catholic College, Sarnen, 1964–1966.*

119. *Church of the Catholic College, Sarnen, ground plan.*

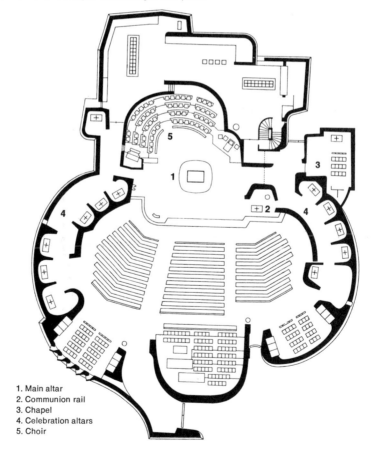

1. Main altar
2. Communion rail
3. Chapel
4. Celebration altars
5. Choir

120. Hans Brutsch: *Catholic church, Buchs, 1966–1968, view from the entrance court.*

121. *Catholic church, Buchs, interior.*

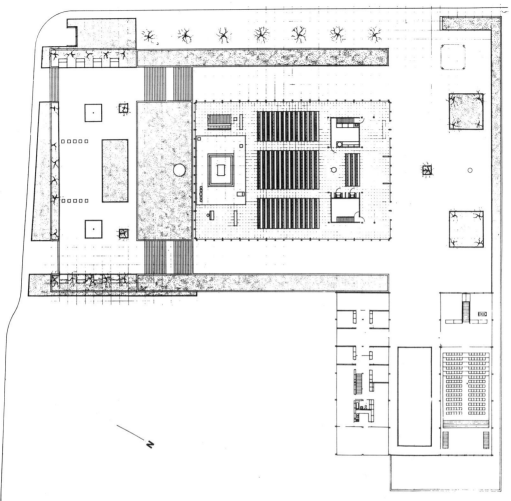

122. *Franz Füeg: Catholic church, Meggen, 1964–1966, ground plan.*

123. *Catholic church, Meggen, view from the south.*

SWITZERLAND: A MODEL CASE?

THIS book covers only a few aspects of current Swiss architecture. All we could attempt was to present some of the most hopeful and most imaginative proposals Swiss architects have to offer within the present building situation.

Architecture itself, this synthesis of technique and art, involves only a few aspects of present Swiss life. Our environment is increasingly determined by elements which lie far from the noble intentions of architects and urban designers, by the supremacy of motor traffic and the shiny spectacles of commercialism in our cities. As elsewhere, the overwhelming percentage of Swiss building is not the result of architectural sensibility, but of the need to coordinate more or less successfully the demand of many people for decent living and working conditions with the demand of individuals or businesses for economic profit.

Architecture is not a goal in itself; Swiss architects are aware of this. Many of them today turn away from formal perfectionism and concentrate their interest on the fundamental socioeconomic processes which underlie the building activity of a mobile, open society that no longer accepts the dictation of an official architectural "style." Is architecture thus becoming more and more superfluous?

Although sociologists may prove that good architecture does not in itself guarantee decent living conditions and happiness, and that architectural ideals may even result in complicating life, it seems that it is through the verities and deficiencies of its architecture that a society on the threshold of a new civilization experiences its problems. Architecture testifies to our often hidden emotional needs and desires and to our ideals. When building reaches the level of architecture it becomes a crystal nucleus irradiating upon its surroundings and into the future and setting new standards.

The day when architecture is identical with life itself will never come. Architecture's great aim, to harmonize and humanize life, will never be fully achieved. But although the models of a harmonious, human life and a harmonious, human society must remain bound to current disorders and malfunctions, it will always be necessary to conceive hypotheses for a better world. This function of architecture reminds us of what technology and economy tend to exclude: the aspiration to goals which lie on a higher plane than everyday requirements of living.

One of the main problems for the future of architecture will be human scale—something, as Max Frisch once noted in his *Tagebuch*, which cannot be altered but can only be lost. It is possible that the small European democracies have an important mission to fulfill toward the humanization of the technological world: to show the possibilities of achieving a certain dignity in the human environment —a dignity which takes into account the past, the root of our existence in nature and society, and which points to a future whose scope will be neither national nor continental but global.

NOTES

1. G. E. Kidder Smith, *The New Architecture of Europe* (New York: World Publishing Company, 1961; London: Pelican Books, 1962), p. 289.
2. Peter Meyer, *Schweizerische Stilkunde* (Zurich: Schweizer Spiegel Verlag, 5th printing, 1944), pp. 203–207.
3. See Werner Blaser's attractive books about Japan, such as *Tempel und Teehaus in Japan* (Olten and Lausanne: Urs Graf-Verlag, 1955) and *Struktur und Gestalt in Japan—Structure and Form in Japan* (Zurich: Artemis-Verlag, 1963).
4. See Nikolaus Pevsner, "The Return of Historicism," *Journal of the Royal Institute of British Architects*, LXVIII (1961).
5. Sigfried Giedion, *Space, Time, and Architecture* (Cambridge, Mass.: Harvard University Press, 5th edition, 1967), p. 24.
6. See Le Corbusier's little-known drawing in which he suggests a spontaneous organization of the facades of his Domino-type, in *Le Corbusier: Oeuvre Complète, 1910–29* (Zurich: Les Editions d'Architecture, 1964), p. 26.
7. Friedrich Achleitner, "Fragen zur Schweizer Architektur," *Bauen Heute* (supplement of the *Berner Tagblatt* [May 15, 1968]).
8. Jane Jacobs, *The Death and Life of Great American Cities* (New York: Random House, 1962).
9. The recent founding of two institutes at the Architectural School of the E.T.H. documents the increasing need for a scientific basis of architectural instruction: the Institut für Geschichte und Theorie der Architektur (Institute for Architectural History and Theory) and the Institut fur Bauforschung (Institute for Scientific Building Research). The former, founded in 1967, is publishing a series of studies on the history and theory of architecture.
10. For more detailed information about Le Corbusier, see Stanislaus von Moos, *Le Corbusier—Elemente einer Synthese* (Frauenfeld and Stuttgart: Verlag Huber, 1968).
11. Sigfried Giedion, *Spatbarocker und romantischer Klassizismus* (Munich: Bruckmann, 1922) and *Bauen in Frankreich: Eisen, Eisenbeton* (Leipzig and Berlin: Klinkhardt und Biermann, 1928).
12. Giedion, *Space, Time, and Architecture*, p. xxxii.
13. *Le Corbusier: Oeuvre Complete, 1934–38* (Zurich: Les Editions d'Architecture, 1964), p. 131.
14. For these figures see the catalogue of the exhibition *Heutige Architektur in der Schweiz* (Swiss Architecture Today), which traveled in Russia in 1968.
15. Karl Ledergerber, *Kunst und Religion in der Verwandlung* (Cologne: DuMont, 1961), p. 14.

BIBLIOGRAPHICAL NOTE

The best documentation of current Swiss architecture is offered by *Werk*, the official periodical of the B.S.A. (Bund Schweizer Architekten), S.W.B. (Schweizerischer Werkbund), and the Schweizerischer Kunstverein. On the sixtieth anniversary of B.S.A. (January, 1968), *Werk* published a special issue covering sixty years of Swiss architecture, a comprehensive but somewhat unsystematic survey. The periodicals *Bauen und Wohnen* (Zurich) and *Architecture, Formes et Fonctions* (Lausanne) are also very informative. Modern architecture in Switzerland up to World War II is best covered in the *M.S.A. (Moderne Schweizer Architektur)—Folder*, compiled by Max Bill (Basel: Karl Werner, 1945). G. E. Kidder Smith's *Switzerland Builds* (Stockholm: Ahlen & Akerlunds Boktryckeri, 1950) still gives the best insight into the standard of everyday Swiss building of the forties. Kidder Smith admirably juxtaposes traditional Swiss native architecture with modern architecture. Another journal, *Architecture d'Aujourd'hui*, has published a special issue on Swiss architecture (June, 1965, No. 121).

The catalogue (in Russian) of the exhibition *Heutige Architektur in der Schweiz* (Swiss Architecture Today) in Moscow in the summer of 1968, is helpful on present-day problems of Swiss architecture. The Foundation Pro Helvetia, which organized the exhibition, has reproduced in German the text of the catalogue, written by planning experts such as Hans Aregger, Jean-Pierre Vouga, and Paul Hofer, and architects such as Charles-Edouard Geisendorf, Alfred Roth, Werner Jegher, and others. A French edition is in preparation. An informative survey of Swiss architecture from 1956–1964 is given by Alfred Altherr in his *New Swiss Architecture* (Teufen: Niggli, 1965). *A Guide to Modern Swiss Architecture* will be published soon by Hans Girsberger and Florian Adler, Zurich.

For more detailed information the following works may be consulted:

General problems
Burckhardt, Lucius, Max Frisch and Markus Kutter. *Achtung: die Schweiz.* Basel: Verlag F. Handschin, 1955.
Burckhardt, Lucius and Walter M. Forderer. *Bauen ein Prozess.* Teufen: Verlag Arthur Niggli, 1968.
Glaus, Otto. *Zurich ohne Zukunft?* Zurich: Verlag für Architektur (Artemis), 1968.
Haller, Fritz. *Integral Urban—a Model.* Olten: Walter-Verlag, 1968.

Work and Traffic

The periodical *Schweizer Journal* is publishing monthly photographs and comments on current Swiss industrial plants and engineering constructions. The yearbook *Der moderne Industriebau in der Schweiz* annually gives a detailed survey.

Bill, Max. *Robert Maillart*. Zurich: Verlag für Architektur (Artemis), 1948.

Housing

Aregger, Hans and Otto Glaus. *Highrise-Building and Urban Design*. Zurich: Verlag für Architektur (Artemis), 1967.

Schools

Roth, Alfred. *The New School*. Zurich: Ed. Girsberger, 1957.

Gross, Roland. "Pädagogischer Schulbau," *Werk* 6 (June, 1963), pp. 209–216.

Churches

Dahinden, Justus. *Bauen für die Kirche in der Welt*. Zurich: NZN-Verlag, 1966.

Förderer, Walter M. *Kirchenbau von heute für morgen?* Zurich: NZN-Verlag, 1964.

Hess, Robert. *Moderne kirchliche Kunst in der Schweiz*. Zurich: NZN-Verlag, 1951.

INDEX

SOURCES OF ILLUSTRATIONS

2. Hans Finsler, Zurich.
3. Leonardo Bezzola, Bätterkinden.
5. Christian Moser, Bern.
7. Otto Pfeifer, Lucerne.
10. Jean Haubensak, Zurich.
12. F. Maurer, Zurich.
15. Fachklasse für Fotographie, Kunstgewerbeschule, Zurich.
16. J. Gasser, Zurich.
17. Peter Grünert, Zurich.
18. Pro Helvetia (Fotodienst), Zurich.
20. G. Ifert, Paris.
21. E. Fehlmann, Burgdorf.
22. Alberto Flammer, Muralto.
26. Jean-Pierre Flury, Lausanne.
27. Leonardo Bezzola, Bätterkinden.
30. G. Klemm, Geneva.
31. Jean Mohr, Geneva.
33. F. Maurer, Zurich.
35. Leonardo Bezzola, Bätterkinden.
37. Dorothee Hess, Zurich.
41. Comet, Zurich.
43. Martin Glaus, Bern.
45. Jean-Pierre Flury, Lausanne.
48. Michael Speich, Winterthur.
49. A. Winkler, Bern.
52. Dieter Rensing, Münster.
54. René Hartmann, Baar.
55. Kurt Amman, Zurich.
58. Oswald Ruppen, Sion.
62. P. Merkle, Basel.
65, 67. Alberto Flammer, Muralto.
69. Comet, Zurich.
71. Peter Grünert, Zurich.
72-73. Jean Mohr, Geneva.
75. Pius Rast, St. Gallen.
77-78. A. Deriaz, Baulmes.
81. Leonardo Bezzola, Bätterkinden.
82. Oswald Ruppen, Sion.
87. Walter Binder, Zurich.
88. Bernhard Moosbrugger, Zurich.
92. Alrège S.A., Lausanne.
95. F. Maurer, Zurich.
96-97. G. Klemm, Geneva.
98, 101. F. Maurer, Zurich.
102. Roger Kaysel, Wettingen.
105. Thomas Cugini, Zurich.
106, 108. F. Maurer, Zurich.
111. Militärflugdienst, Dübendorf.
112. Jean Haubensak, Zurich.
118. Lorenz Fischer, Lucerne.
120. Peter Ammon, Lucerne.
123. Bernhard Moosbrugger, Zurich.